To
Mary Kate,
I hope you
enjoy it.

Steve Joynt

JACK'S LAW

THE RISE AND FALL OF RENEGADE JUDGE JACK MONTGOMERY

STEVE JOYNT

CRANE HILL
PUBLISHERS

Birmingham, Alabama

Printed in the United States of America
Published by Crane Hill Publishers

Library of Congress Cataloging-in-Publication Data

Joynt, Steve.
   Jack's law : the rise and fall of renegade judge Jack Montgomery / by
Steve Joynt. — 1st ed.
      p.   cm.
   ISBN 1-881548-40-6
   1. Montgomery, Jack, 1930-1994. 2. Judges — Alabama — Biography.
I. Title.
KF373.M554J33   1996
340'.092 — dc20
[B]   96-24236
                                                               CIP

10   9   8   7   6   5   4   3   2   1

Dedicated to
my mother, Joy Joynt,
for giving me my sense of humor and creativity,
and
my father, Richard G. "Sweetie Pie" Joynt,
for not encouraging me to become a lawyer
and not discouraging me from becoming a writer.

"When I'm gone, I sure don't want anybody
putting up a picture of me to hang
in the courtroom like those other guys in there.
I don't need that. I don't even care
how I'm remembered. When I'm dead,
you can say anything about me. I don't care.
I'll be gone."

Jack Montgomery, 1985

TABLE OF CONTENTS

INTRODUCTION

I have to admit it. I liked Jack Montgomery. As a newspaper reporter who made at least a few trips to his courtroom, I always found it amusing to watch Judge Montgomery create chaos among the assembled attorneys simply for the fun of watching them jump. Whenever I interviewed him, he always demonstrated that he understood what reporters wanted: a good quote without a lot of technical jargon. I usually had to beg him to clean up his language so that I could quote him in the paper, but that was his way of making reporters jump. He knew good and well that he couldn't be quoted in the newspaper as long as he peppered his speech with "shit" and much worse; he was just showing off, daring us to quote him in full. Usually, though, I appreciated that he was not afraid to speak from his gut, and the memorable quotes rolled off his tongue.

But that was all I knew about Jack Montgomery. He was a big, crazy-ass guy, a man's man who might punch you in the mouth and ask questions later. In the legal world, governed by gray, stodgy old men and their dusty rules, Jack was a Tasmanian devil.

Later, when I was assigned to cover the federal bribery case against Jack, I started to learn much more about his behavior in his courtroom and the events in his personal life. For the most part, it wasn't pretty, but it was as fascinating as a twenty-car pileup. The more I learned, the more I wanted to find out. I was riveted by this old man and fascinated by the way he was able to get away with everything he did.

Do I still like him? I'm not sure. I do feel sorry for him, but I also feel sorry for some of the people he came in contact with, especially the ones he married.

While I was doing the research for this book, people occasionally asked me, "Why a book about Jack Montgomery?" It was a fair question. Why was old Jack book material? He did not write any law. He did not set any precedents. Mostly, he accepted guilty pleas and meted out sentences or sent cases along to the grand jury. Many felt that while he was highly unorthodox, to say the least, he usually made good horse-sense decisions. That was Jack's saving grace, actually, the fact that most of his decisions were sound. He was that rare kind of judge who could sometimes make both sides in a case go away feeling like justice had been done.

At other times, though, folks said that "miscarriage of justice" was not a strong enough term to describe what happened in Jack Montgomery's courtroom. Nobody ever seemed to listen to those people, though.

Lawyers and judges who work in the criminal system are, as a whole, a funny breed. Nobody, except cops, comes in more contact with criminals, creeps, and scumbags than lawyers and judges do. Every day they hear and see the worst things mankind is capable of doing, and they usually hear that the victims and witnesses never saw it coming. Witnesses often say, "He was the nicest man you'd ever want to know, until he slaughtered his whole family."

And yet these lawyers and judges never seem to think the members of their own club are capable of any wrongdoing. "Fred? You mean Fred the prosecutor? I know him. I've faced him in court plenty of times, had lunch with him twice. He's a great guy. No way could Fred be crooked."

Maybe that's human nature. We don't want to think that people who are like us can be bad. That's how Jack was able to get away with things for so long. His colleagues made excuses for him, and some even admired him. Others were afraid of him or simply frustrated by the system built on the premise of that quirk of human nature.

As a judge and a person, Jack Montgomery was loud and crude, sometimes even violent. He was egocentric and selfish. In Jack's courtroom, it was said that anyone who walked in there was no longer subject simply to the laws of the State of Alabama, they were subject to Jack's Law—which could take the form of whatever mood he was in or whatever level his fickle blood-sugar level sank to. No one ever knew what he might do. He might treat a defendant like a kindly grandpa would or come down on him like the wrath of the Almighty Himself.

From one perspective, Jack was colorful. He refused to wear judicial robes, preferring instead his flashy sport coats. Fire-engine red one day, mind-numbing plaid the next. He always had at least one gun with him at all times, usually two, and thought it great fun to pull one out and point it at someone every now and then. He never did anything in moderation: He married five times. His last wife was half his age. He once set the world's highest bond. He always flew through his docket in a few hours and went home by lunch.

From another perspective, Jack was a drunk, a liar, and a crook. Those are strong words that most people refrained from using, but I believe they fit. He was an alcoholic, which played incredible havoc with his brittle diabetes. He told tall tales about himself, self-aggrandizing stuff that made him appear even more macho than he was. And in the end he took the job he always said he'd "fight a forty-foot gorilla" to keep, and he urinated on it. He extorted money from some of the defendants who appeared in his court. In exchange, he lowered their bonds or tried to make their cases go away.

But I think the best word that I have heard to describe Jack embraces both perspectives: Jack was a bully. He liked to push people around. He tested them. If they wilted, then they didn't measure up. If they met him on his own ground, he liked them. If they stood up to him, he backed down. And like all bullies, he was usually the most insecure person in the room. He tested you so that you wouldn't test him. He displayed emotions but never shared them. Jack always spoke his mind but never spoke his heart.

I think the real tragedy of Jack's life was that he never let anyone in to help him, and he had always been in need of help. Jack, though, did not grow up in a time or place where men of substance asked for help. He came from the great Age of Internalization. On the outside, he built a huge, cussing, gun-toting, fire-breathing monster of a judge. That was to hide the shattered kid from backwater Louisiana who did not know how to love himself or anyone else. No one could get in, and Jack could not get out. Most of his wives said they never really knew Jack.

For many of his almost eighteen years on the bench, people in and around Birmingham were captivated by Jack. Whether in print or on TV, he could always be counted on to say or do something outlandish. My colleagues and I, the media, were as much to blame as anyone else for building the legend and ignoring the real person. Many of us knew that his antics often stepped far beyond what should be considered proper behavior for a judge, but like a lot of the attorneys and other judges, we chuckled, shook our heads, and said, "That's Jack." When Jack wanted, he could be the world's most likable guy, and we all liked him. The media took him to task a few times, but it always seemed to roll off his back.

For the few who had to do business in his courtroom and were outraged by his behavior, there was little they could do.

The brethren of the bench is one of the last great vestiges of good ole boyism. Sure, there's an organization charged with overseeing judges, but it's run largely by lawyers and judges. The most that ever happened to Jack before the feds caught him doing something truly illegal was a slight slap to the wrist.

When the feds did haul him into court and charge him with racketeering and extortion, we and his public were shaken to say the least. Frankly we knew he was nuts, but we always thought he was honest. Once touted as the "Slamming Judge" who said that his politics were "three clicks to the right of Attila the Hun," he turned out to be what he supposedly despised the most, one of the bad guys. And as was typical of anything connected with Jack, the prosecution of the case against him was filled with bizarre twists and turns, ending with a bang, not a whimper: his unsolved death by a gunshot.

So many people wanted to know why he did it—why he befouled the very thing that gave him so much notoriety. Of course only Jack could have said for sure why he did it, but I believe this book will point the reader to a couple of conclusions. First of all, taking bribe money was not as shocking as it appeared from the outside. It was not that far of a leap from the personal justice he had been executing for years. And he did seem to be in the habit of doing favors for lawyer friends. Why not get paid for it for a change? Second, the man who decided to commit these crimes was wracked with health problems and substance abuse. His head was full of lifelong demons seen through an alcohol-induced fog. Third, while he was not in deep trouble fiscally, he had a young wife he adored and wanted to spoil, but he didn't have much cash on hand. He had always spent money just a little faster than it came in, so a little more certainly came in handy.

My personal belief is that while Jack knew he was committing crimes against the system, he had left that system a long time before. He had nothing but contempt for the intricacies, details, and technicalities of criminal justice. Three years, ten years, parole, probation: It was all such a load of horseshit to him. The real criminals should be sent away for good or killed; the others should be turned loose. Just haul a guy before him, and he could figure out what to do. Jack fancied himself to be more like a wilderness judge who sat on his front porch and issued decisions after stroking his chin for a minute. He didn't need the wild legalistic ramblings of the state legislature to figure out right and wrong. The issue of bond, for example, was so arbitrary. There were recommended levels of bond, but no judge stuck to those. One judge might set a $500,000 bond one day, and a different judge might release the same defendant on his own recognizance the next day. If you're going to lower a dope dealer's bond, Jack probably thought, why not make him pay for the privilege? In the end the system will probably not punish him nearly as much as he ought to be punished, so why not drain his pockets now? That's punishment—that's what hurts a drug dealer.

So the original question stands. Why write a book about such a reprehensible, small-time judge?

Anyone who is interested in the judicial system or in people who rise to power needs to know the story of Jack Montgomery. He was one of the few people we select to sit in judgment on us and to protect us from each other. We somehow allowed him to prostitute that highest of trusts. He slipped through the cracks by fooling us all. But we invited him to fool us. We liked being fooled.

Besides, I think most of us have an innate fascination with the scoundrels in our midst. They always seem to get away with things we wish we could do. To whatever else that should be said about Jack Montgomery, add this: He lived life exactly the way he wanted to. He was not unconventional on purpose—he was himself on purpose. When Jack went to a store and was mistreated in some way by the clerk behind the counter, he did not walk out muttering, "I shouldn't have said, 'Thank you very much'—I should have said, 'Shove it up your ass.' " Jack said what he felt at all times. Call that a lack of socialization or just plain rudeness, but we can't help but wish sometimes that we were not so socialized.

This story is not without a few heroes either. From the scared young cop who dared to question the actions of this truly scary judge to the seasoned FBI agent who used his considerable wits to catch the cagey old guy in the act, there is reaffirmation here that the system works, eventually. Jack, we hope, was an aberration. The events that led to his eventual exposure were the natural course of business carried on largely by dedicated and dutiful people.

Above all, the story of Jack Montgomery is just that—a good story. I can only hope that I've been able to do it justice.

CHAPTER ONE

GOD, I HATE DOING THAT

Friday morning. Judge Jack Montgomery strode into his courtroom shortly after nine o'clock. He was rarely right on time. Why should he be punctual? Nothing could start without him. He absentmindedly patted his side, reassuring himself that his gun was in its holster. He had gotten almost no sleep last night, and he just wanted to get through this day and figure out what to do next. The usual bustle of the Jefferson County District Court was all around him as he slowly stepped up to his bench. He felt the comfort of his cushioned swivel chair as he dropped himself into it. He looked around the bench for a moment. This was where he belonged, he assured himself. He looked at the files in front of him, attempting to immerse himself in the details of the day.

Pushing sixty-three, Jack still was a good-looking man with a square jaw and ruddy complexion. His hair was thinning and snowy white, but that just made his icy blue eyes look brighter. He was an imposing figure. He stood six feet two inches tall and still looked trim. He had the build of a linebacker with the kind of long arms that could reach halfway across the field and pull anyone down with a single yank. He looked as though he were made of granite, and he struck fear into defendants with just a glance.

District court is where all felony cases begin. Initial appearances, where defendants either present their attorneys to the court or have attorneys assigned to them, are held there.

Preliminary hearings, also held in district court, come next in the process, where a sketch of the evidence is given through testimony so the judge can determine if the case should be sent to the grand jury. Once a district judge passes the case, it's out of his hands. Motions concerning bond and guilty pleas are also handled in district court. If the defendant decides to plead guilty right then, the district judge pronounces sentence and disposes of the case, usually along the lines of a plea agreement hashed out by the prosecutor and the defense. District court is the distribution center of the Alabama criminal justice system. And here in the largest county in Alabama, which included the largest city, Birmingham, district court stays damn busy.

Friday was plea day, when the judge heard from those defendants who wanted to plead guilty and pronounced their sentences. Deputy District Attorney Bill Neuman sat in the witness stand as he often did, shuffling through the day's files, figuring out what had to be done and in what order. As the defendants' names riffled past his eyes, Neuman's mind was on the Auburn University football game he was going to attend the next day. On an autumn Friday in the state of Alabama, it's hard for anyone to keep his mind on anything but football. Neuman wasn't worried about being tied up in court too long, though. He'd be able to make the 150-mile trip to The Plains of Auburn with time to spare. He knew Jack wouldn't go past lunch—he never did. The old man could charge through a docket. Regardless of the issues, Jack always wrapped up by lunch and always chewed through the twenty to twenty-five cases lined up for that day. Neuman had been in the DA's office about eighteen years, the last two in Jack's court. His time here had taken some of the life out of him, though. He was serving a sentence of his own, sharing his cell with a maniac.

Jack was a courthouse legend, nothing less. Some people are legends for good reasons—Jack was not. He was an insulin-dependent diabetic who obviously didn't pay much attention to regulating his blood sugar. To make matters worse, he drank—he drank a lot, and everyone knew it. His bailiffs became experts at recognizing a low blood-sugar attack and simply brought the judge a Coke when they saw one coming on. That would not be so bad, except Jack was ornery even when his blood-sugar level was perfect. Catch him on a bad day, and he'd start screaming and tossing papers into the air for no reason at all. He might even pull out his gun. On a good day, Jack delighted in giving attorneys a hard time and making the gallery laugh with his filthy language and caustic, off-color, sometimes even racist remarks. The doctrine of political correctness never crossed this judge's desk.

Neuman had heard the stories before he was assigned to Jack, and he'd been in Jack's court on a few occasions before. But he also knew that the judge had taken a turn for the worst in the last year or so. One day in court, in the middle of the proceedings, Jack suddenly became very quiet. Then he slammed his huge fist down on the bench and shouted, "Damn!" Then he just stared at the back wall of the court-room for a long time. Another time, after a shouting match with Attorney Hiram Dodd, Jack told Dodd he never wanted to see him in his courtroom again. Sometimes Jack just flat lost his place in the proceedings. His erratic behavior was increasingly becoming bizarre and worrisome behavior.

Neuman was a soft-spoken, unassuming prosecutor. He had seen other attorneys do battle with Jack and often win, but they had the luxury of escaping. They didn't have to come back and deal with him day after day. No, in his situation, placating, even baby-sitting the judge seemed like the best approach for Neuman—although the idea of private practice was starting to look pretty good to him.

On this particular Friday, Peggy Sanford, a reporter for *The Birmingham News*, was among those in the courtroom gallery. That wasn't terribly unusual. Even though felony trials weren't held in district court, reporters sometimes came by to get a first look at a defendant in a notorious case, or if things were slow, they would simply stop in trolling for stories. Jack's courtroom was usually good for something. He'd say or do something outrageous, sometimes because he knew the media was there, and it would be a funny little bright in the paper the next day. But on this morning, Sanford knew about something big. By the looks of things, she knew something that nobody else in the court knew. She had gotten a tip the night before. She had even driven over to Jack's house that night, but apparently she had arrived too late—the place was dark. So she had planned to run through the courthouse and see what she could find out this morning. She certainly didn't expect to see Jack holding court as usual, so she found a bench and waited to see what was going to happen next.

Jack hadn't been on the bench more than ten minutes or so and was still shuffling papers and talking with his bailiffs, when Circuit Judge James Hard, a respected, no-nonsense guy who had the makings of a real jurist, stuck his head into the courtroom from the back entrance. Circuit judges sit above district judges and essentially outrank them. Hard was amazed to see Jack in his usual place, after what he had just heard. Minutes ago Hard had been in the U.S. Attorney's office getting confirmation of the phone call he had received from a friend the night before. Hard asked at the federal office that morning, "Was it as bad as it sounded?" It was worse than he'd thought, he quickly found out. Hard leaned up to Jack and whispered, "I'd like to see you in your chambers. Now."

Without a word Jack stood up and followed Hard out of the courtroom. Neuman didn't think anything of it. Two minutes later Jack came back into the courtroom and curtly told his bailiffs to remove everyone and lock the doors. Then he walked back into his chambers and locked the door behind him. Oh well, Neuman thought, who knows? It was always something with Jack. And he walked back to his office.

Sanford, though, realized that Hard knew what happened. She ran up to his office to interview him, but he wasn't there. She waited. After a few minutes, Steve Visser, another reporter for the *News* found Sanford in Hard's office. He had been briefed on what was going on, and Sanford told him to stake out Jack's office.

In the newsroom of WBRC-TV Channel 6, someone received an anonymous phone call that simply said something important was going on in Jack's courtroom. That was all the assignment desk needed to hear. Reporter Michael Jones was sent there with cameraman Scott Lukich. When they got to the courthouse, they saw that Jack's door was closed and Visser was hanging around. Visser wasn't exactly pleased to see the TV guys. Up until now, he was pretty sure he and Sanford had the scoop on a big story. Jones raised his hand to knock on the door when Visser said, "Don't do that—you might piss him off. Who knows what he'll do?"

Jones shrugged and wandered back out into the hallway to see what he could find out. Why on earth was he here anyway? A few minutes later Jack opened the door of his small chambers. Visser said, "Judge, can I ask you a couple of questions?" Jack, startled for a second, looked at Visser and said, "Come in here," gesturing inside the door.

Jack spotted Jones and Lukich in the hallway and told his bailiff to bring the TV guys in too. "Oh, God," Visser first thought. "He's going to kill himself on TV." He also couldn't help but think what a great story that would be.

Lukich set up his camera on a tripod and zoomed in on Jack sitting behind his desk. Jones took a seat and waited to see what was going to unfold. "This is my resignation, dated October 23, 1992," Jack said. "A carbon copy will be sent to Governor Guy Hunt," and he handed the paper to a bailiff for copies to be made.

"Why are you resigning, Judge?" Visser asked.

"Because it's time," Jack said, leaning back. "There's a time for everything. I hit the wall. Did you ever do something so long that you can't do it anymore? I've been coming apart. I've been feeling bad, feeling sick. I'm not in the best health anymore. Wendy's not going to like it. A lot of other people are going to like it."

Resigning for health reasons seemed reasonable enough, Jones thought. The end of a long, colorful, sometimes turbulent career. This story would probably take all day, gathering reaction from lawyers and judges, going through old tapes.

"Are you in trouble, Judge?" Visser asked.

"I'm always in trouble," Jack said with a laugh.

"With law enforcement?"

"Not yet. I don't know that I won't be sometime."

Was Visser just fishing? Jones wondered.

"I've lived in this business for a long time," Jack said. "I have three live death threats against me right now. It gets kind of on your nerves after a while. It's time to get it over with. It's over. About four o'clock this morning, I was lying awake deciding that."

"Did the police visit you at home last night?" Visser asked him.

"No. Did they visit you?" Jack retorted. "Oh," he said, waving his hand as if it weren't important, "they had been by a couple of times looking for a guy who supposedly was hiding out a few houses down from me. I had my shotgun on them until they showed me their badges."

Visser knew something, Jones thought. Something was definitely going on. This was not a graceful exit for health reasons, and the story was looking a lot more complicated.

The bailiff returned with the copies of the resignation letter. Jack told him to stand by. He picked up his pen, looked down at the desk, and emitted a low moan. Then he signed the letters. "God, I hate doing that," he said as the bailiff removed the papers. "I want to, and I hate to." Tears were rolling out of his tired eyes. "I gotta take a break. I can't handle it anymore. I can't handle it." He took a sip from a can of caffeine-free Coke.

"Is this a case of entrapment, Judge?" Visser asked.

Jack laughed. "Ask the right questions, Visser, for Christ's sake."

"Were the police searching your house last night?" the reporter asked.

"They can if they wish," Jack said. "They can come over there any time they want. They've all been there enough times. They know my house better than I know my house.

"This is going to hit me sometime today. I'm proud of the job I did, and I'm sorry for the things I've done that were wrong."

With that, Jones and Lukich packed up their gear. Still stunned that Jack would do this on camera when he was obviously in some kind of serious trouble, Jones simply stuck out his hand and told Jack to take care of himself.

Visser stuck around, but Jack left a couple of minutes later to go see his attorney, Mark White.

"Now everybody can talk bad about me because I've resigned," Jack said as he walked away.

Minutes later, as White later testified, Jack, someone White had considered to be a friend for many years, showed up in his office, trembling and almost incoherent. "The feds are after me," was about all Jack could tell him. White called the U.S. Attorney's office and got the rundown: FBI agents had searched Jack's home in suburban Vestavia Hills the night before and recovered thousands of dollars in marked bribe money. White took Jack home, and it did not take the attorney long to surmise that his friend was a wreck. He found pill bottles of anabolic steroids and the powerful antidepressant Xanax and who knew what else. When he asked Jack about the specifics of the search, all Jack could say was, "They were here. The agents were here," and then he'd start mumbling. Jack finally broke down and started talking about killing himself. White set about getting him some psychological help.

That afternoon the story was out. Jack Montgomery, the Slamming Judge, that tough-talking, pistol-packing bastion of right versus wrong, had resigned because federal agents were investigating him for taking bribes.

CHAPTER TWO

JACKIE BOY

The record shows that John Henry Montgomery Jr. was born on Christmas Eve 1930 in the New Orleans apartment of Lillian Jeffers on Crete Street, just below the state fairgrounds. His mother, according to the birth certificate, was Mrs. Violet Jeffers Montgomery, and his father was John Henry Montgomery, who lived in Tickfaw, Louisiana, a little bitty town about fifty miles north of New Orleans. Jack Montgomery's birth certificate was not filled out on the day of his birth because he was not born in a hospital. Instead, his parents swore to the above information before a magistrate more than three months after Jack's birth. They did that on April Fool's Day, actually, in 1931. Years later Jack said the joke was on him.

There are several aspects of Jack Montgomery's life that remain question marks, mostly because he told so many versions of the truth that the truth is nearly impossible to discern. Sometimes his version seemed to fly in the face of the available documentation, but like any truly skillful liar, he always accounted for that. The circumstances of his birth remain nearly as mysterious as the circumstances of his death. Looking at the record, it all seems pretty clear. Violet Montgomery was his mother. She gave birth at her sister's place. Her sister was a registered nurse.

After his mother died in 1986, however, Jack supposedly discovered the truth of his birth. He told varying versions of this truth. At times he told people that he never knew his parents, that he was adopted or that his father wasn't really his father. Sometimes he said that his mother had appeared to him as an apparition shortly after her death and revealed the truth to him. Other times he said family records he found in her home gave him the story. His most detailed account usually went along the lines of the tale he told a couple of FBI agents one night. "I thought I knew who my parents were, but I really don't," he said. "I grew up with two people who claimed to be my parents. I figured out that my virgin aunt had a torrid love affair, and I'm the product of that. She gave me to her sister, and she raised me." Lillian, he said, couldn't stand the pain of the illegitimate birth because of her strict Catholic upbringing.

It all seems quite plausible. Lillian, the younger of the sisters, had moved from Minnesota to New Orleans. She would not have been the first single woman to fall under the spell of a man amidst the charm and romance of the Crescent City. In 1930, though, illegitimate births were things that families tried desperately to disguise. Entire lives were rearranged, even ruined, to keep those kinds of things secret. One way to keep the secret was to give birth at home rather than go to a hospital, where they kept records. Would it be inconceivable for the older sister, Violet, who was thirty-two at the time, married, and had a daughter, to help her younger sister out of a life-ruining situation and simply volunteer to take her illegitimate nephew and raise him as her own? In those days, it was not. And such a thing would probably be kept secret from the child, at least until he was old enough to handle the truth.

And while it certainly wasn't unheard of for a thirty-two-year-old woman and her thirty-four-year-old husband to give birth to their second child almost ten years after their first, it was a bit unusual. Jack didn't look much like his parents either. While his father was short and stocky, Jack grew tall and lean, all the way up to six foot two.

On the other hand, a child who was not fond of his parents could certainly create fantasies about his "real" parents. These were not his real parents at all. Maybe the president was really his father. His aunt was probably his mother. She seemed nice. Who are these people who claim to be his parents? Obviously a number of unhappy children have daydreamed that they were really orphans, even to the point of convincing themselves that it was true. Jack, though, was not a child when he began to tell the supposedly complete story of his parentage. Until his mother's death, he let it be known that he did not like his father, but he never questioned the man's claim to paternal rights.

Jack, who was called Jackie Boy by everyone in his family, was raised in the sparse wooden Montgomery home in Tickfaw, Louisiana. They were not well-off but not dirt-poor either. Violet Montgomery worked as a housemother for dormitories and fraternity houses at Southeastern Louisiana College, which is now a university, in nearby Hammond. It was a live-in job, so she was rarely home. Jack's father was a rural postal carrier who, Jack later claimed, worked the longest rural route in the country.

Jack claimed that his father was a heavy drinker who buried his bottles in the backyard, thinking no one would know about his drinking if the evidence was not in plain sight. Jack had told at least four of his wives and many other people over the years that his father physically abused him in terrible ways. His father would go into drunken rages and tie young Jack to trees and beat him with a bullwhip or a razor strap, as Jack told it. Left alone for days at a time, Jack said he had to search for food in the nearby river or beg neighbors for meals. Whether or not this was true,

Jack's father seemed to be a constant source of emotional pain in Jack's life, even after his father's death in 1972.

Jack's sister, Nelda Montgomery Stillman, refused to be interviewed by the media about Jack or his childhood. She did tell FBI agents that Jack lied about her father and that Jack's childhood was normal and happy.

Family friends, however, said that Nelda used to refer to her father as "the beast." Jack claimed his sister left home in her teen years, leaving her much younger brother to literally fend for himself against "the beast." Could Jack have been exaggerating to get sympathy? Could Nelda have been exaggerating to save herself the embarrassment of admitting that she came from a highly dysfunctional home and the guilt of leaving her much younger brother alone with their abuser? Either seems equally plausible.

If, however, Jack had been lying about his father all those years, his actions on August 24, 1990, seem quite puzzling. On that day, nearly twenty years after his father died, Judge John Henry Montgomery Jr. went to a Jefferson County magistrate, paid an $11 legal fee, and had his name changed to Jack Montgomery. Why bother? That's the name he had been using exclusively for nearly thirty years. He didn't even sign official records as John Henry Montgomery Jr. anymore. No one but he and the magistrate would ever even know that it was legally changed.

"It was an exorcism," Jack's fifth wife and widow, Wendy Williams, said. "He didn't want that name anymore. He walked over there and did it himself. It was like a triumph for him. He was trying to make himself right."

Jack only had one child, Jeffrey, who was born to Jack's first wife, Ruth. Jack abandoned his wife and son when Jeff was only seven. Through four more wives, Jack made it clear that he did not want to be a father. His wives believed that Jack was afraid of being a father—even more, he was afraid of becoming his father. Over the years Jack stayed in touch with his son, but only in a way one might keep in touch with an old college buddy: a present on his birthday, a phone call every now and then. Ironically Jeff grew into the kind of man who believes strongly in the importance of family and fatherhood. Being a father, he once said, is the most important part of his life.

So Jack hated his father. That's not so unusual, and that doesn't mean his father beat him with whips or neglected him. But several people who were closest to Jack over the years and several psychologists who examined him near the end of his life all said that the tales of abuse were among the few things Jack said about his early life that they truly believed.

"I knew his father," Jack's second wife, Phyllis, said. Her description of the man was succinct but corroborative: "He was an asshole."

Jack's fourth wife, Jennifer, rose to the level of captain in the Jefferson County Sheriff's office. Along the way she became a skilled investigator with a special talent for working with victims, especially kids. "The more I learned about victimology and how child victims act as adults, the more I came to believe that Jack was abused as a child. Badly abused."

Jack finished Natalberry Grammar School in Tangipahoa Parish in March 1944 and then entered Hammond High School. He was one of the country kids who had to take the long bus ride into town every morning. Don Sibley was a friend of Jack's in high school. They hung out together in a small pack that included Sibley's future wife, Jo, and Jack's future first wife, Ruth. "Jack was everybody's friend, but he wasn't really close to anyone," Sibley said. "Even then, it seemed to be difficult for him to have any kind of real relationship."

Jack was a tall, good-looking young man. He didn't play any sports, but he was certainly built for it. He was a cutup, the kind of kid who had to be the center of attention. "He was ambitious but never very studious," Sibley said. "He was kind of a buffoon, and he could always make people laugh." But he could be confrontational too, always enjoying a good argument. And he tested people, talking crudely. "He could offend the hell out of you if you didn't know him," Sibley said. "He was always cynical about human relationships. I don't think he put his faith in anybody."

Sibley recalled that Jack had no respect for his father, and Sibley had always gotten the impression that there was a big secret lurking somewhere in Jack's family. From what Sibley knew of Jack's father, "Mr. Henry" as folks called him, he "was sort of a ne'er-do-well."

Jack graduated from high school in January 1949. He left home to spend more than a year working for the Shell Oil Company, as so many young men in Louisiana did. The oil business in the gulf was booming, and the companies were a solid source of employment.

He returned to Hammond in the fall of 1950 to start college where his mother worked, Southeastern Louisiana. But in less than a year, Jack joined the army with dreams of becoming an officer, going to Korea, and coming back a hero.

CHAPTER THREE

PRISONER OF WAR

They parachuted in at night miles behind enemy lines, a small band of American soldiers trained to kill with their bare hands as well as a variety of weapons, sent on a secret reconnaissance mission. Jack Montgomery had been in Korea only a short time, and now he was creeping along through the woods at night, his weapon at the ready, the adrenaline pumping so hard that he could hear it. He could also hear the night creatures chirping in trees all around him. No matter how softly he tried to walk, the crunch of leaves and twigs under his feet seemed too loud. At times the point man would raise one hand and they would all stop and crouch, eyes wide, hearts pounding. When they were certain there was no danger ahead, they resumed their mission.

Finally Jack felt like he was doing something significant. He wasn't just fighting a war—he was leading the way, penetrating enemy territory to carry out an act of sabotage against the enemy. If he were lucky, he'd have the chance for some hand-to-hand combat. He was ready. All those afternoons spent as a boy in the Louisiana swamps foraging for crawfish and freshwater mussels were finally coming in handy. He knew how to live off the land, how to sneak through the woods without being heard. Korea wasn't so bad. The mosquitoes in Louisiana were much worse. So was the heat.

Then it happened—the barrage of gunfire practically exploded in their faces. A patrol of Chinese regulars had been waiting for them and executed its ambush perfectly. Hell, these guys had probably been watching from the time the Special Forces team jumped out of their plane. Jack and the others jumped to whatever cover they could find and started firing back, but it was useless. Several of the Americans were killed right there. The remaining few, including Jack, had no choice but to surrender as the dozen or so Chinese soldiers moved in on them.

With their hands on their heads, the small crew of Americans was marched through the darkness, deeper into Communist territory. They were taken to the base camp of the soldiers, where they were questioned and beaten, one at a time, for nearly a week. Their captors knew that the Americans were an elite squad sent in to conduct a highly classified mission. When it was clear, though, that the Americans were not going to say anything, the Chinese soldiers had them sent to the nearest prisoner of war camp. The intelligence soldiers at the camp, being better trained at conducting torturous interrogations, would surely have more success extracting information from the uncooperative American soldiers.

At the camp, time for the Americans was measured in increments of torture. A minute, a day, it didn't mean much. For them there were two times: pain and when the pain stopped. For a few there was death. The prisoners were starved and beaten. Deprived of sleep, they spent hours, even days, tied to chairs under white hot lights, their captors tirelessly questioning them over and over in English and Chinese. When the weather got cold, the Chinese were fond of selecting a prisoner, stripping him, strapping him naked to a metal gurney, and leaving him outside. Occasionally they would spray water on him so it would freeze overnight. Prisoners lost fingers and toes to frostbite. Sometimes a prisoner would be tied to a tree and whipped relentlessly while their captors kicked them, spit on them, and screamed at them.

Jack and the other Americans stayed alive by supplementing their food with the ants, roaches, and rats they were able to catch. Instead of sleeping during the moments when the Chinese left them alone, the Americans talked about escape plans. They sharpened a few spoons and started digging through the dirt floor of their pen.

One night, after months in this man-made hell, they broke through with their spoons. They sneaked past the guards and slipped into the woods. They were giddy with freedom but wracked with fatigue, sickness, and hunger. For three days they wandered, until they realized they had walked in a circle and had come back to the prison camp. In tears of frustration, the small band of Americans made one final, desperate plan. They decided on a sneak attack: Take the guards out quietly, one by one, gathering weapons as they went along. Mustering what little strength they could, slowly, stealthily, they ambushed the guards and killed them. By morning the camp was theirs. They turned the other prisoners loose and put the few guards they captured into the holding pens. They filled their bellies on the guards' food, packed knapsacks and maps, and made their way back to the front until they found an American unit on patrol.

Everyone who knew Jack later in his life realized that this experience had profoundly affected him, changed him, and perhaps explained why he was such a volatile person. There were the obvious signs, like how he absolutely refused ever to eat in a Chinese restaurant, regardless of who invited him. And how he avoided anyone who looked even remotely Asian. He often slipped into casual conversation that he was in Korea or that he'd been a prisoner of war, but he did not go into much detail unless it was a one-on-one conversation and he was in the mood. Whenever he told it, the person who heard it was awestruck by the brutality Jack endured and the odds he overcame to escape. And he told it in such vivid detail.

The only problem is that it never happened.

Not one single word of it is true. OK, he was in the military—that much is true. But the closest he ever got to Korea was a base in Hawaii. He was not in the Special Forces, he never fired a shot at an enemy soldier, and he was certainly never held captive by the Chinese.

According to his military records, Jack enlisted for a three-year hitch in the army in April 1951. After basic training, he was stationed in Oahu. Then he signed up for Officer Candidate School and was sent to Fort Benning, Georgia. There it was discovered that Jack suffered from brittle diabetes, also known as juvenile diabetes, the most severe form of the disease. For the rest of his life, he would have to regulate his blood-sugar level with diet and insulin. He was sent from Fort Benning to Fort Hood, Texas, where he could be treated at the hospital facility. Since the seriousness of his diabetes prevented Jack from any form of military service, he received a disability discharge in January 1953 as a private. He was given a severance pay of $889.20 and a travel allowance of $30.

Like any experienced liar, Jack had an explanation for what the records would say if anyone ever went to the trouble of looking them up. He told his wives that his mission was so secret that his records would never reflect his imprisonment or even the fact that he was in Korea. He operated under so many fake names that even he didn't know what to call himself anymore.

It wasn't a bad cover story. This was the military after all, and the military was capable of keeping any secret it wanted to, right? At least three of his wives believed his story, and all of his friends and colleagues did. It seemed to fit.

But years later as the FBI went through every detail of Jack's life, they quickly found that there simply could not have been any truth to the story. When a magazine article was written about Jack in 1985, he made no mention of his hardship to the reporter. The story said he had joined the army and then quoted Jack as saying he was "no great hero, just your run-of-the-mill GI."

Why would a POW with such an incredible story not tell it for a magazine article? Perhaps he got a sudden bout of discretion and decided that it was one thing to tell a real whopper to everyone he knew, but it was something again to repeat it for print. If he spread it too far, he figured, someone might call his bluff. As it was, other judges who were Korean War veterans sometimes tried to engage him in conversation and found that he was unfamiliar with very basic information about various American units or places in Korea. A successful liar knows how far to take the lie and where to stop. If someone close to him asked why he didn't tell the reporter about his time in Korea, he could always say he was just being humble. After all, it was a classified mission—no sense getting the army on his case after all of those years.

Then one is left with the question of why someone would make up such an incredible story. Self-aggrandizement is the easy answer. There was no denying that people were impressed when they heard the story. They admired Jack for his sacrifice and felt a little sorry for him. They made allowances for him. If he invented it to simply get a little more attention, to keep people off balance in his presence, and to make himself seem a little more like John Wayne, then it worked perfectly.

That simple answer, however, does not address the deeper questions involved in this incredible lie. Why and how was Jack able to attach so much emotional significance to this fable that it even affected him in his sleep? For several years he would wake up screaming from the nightmares about his captors.

And why did he develop not only such detail, but such humiliating tortures as part of his story? If someone was just making it up, one would think they'd throw in some beatings and bright lights, but strapped down naked on a metal gurney, sprayed with water, and left to freeze outside? Sometimes when he told the story, it ended with the Americans not only killing but eating the Chinese soldiers. It had developed into the kind of story one did not necessarily tell with pride. It was more like a deep, dark secret that he admitted in private moments. In 1987, nearly thirty years after his supposed captivity, Jack was diagnosed with post-traumatic stress disorder, a result of being a prisoner of war, and he was prescribed Xanax. He even fooled the doctors.

According to psychologists, victims of child abuse sometimes transfer the hurt and the humiliation of their abuse into an entirely different and more socially acceptable setting. A fantastic story about how they were attacked by wild dogs or even beaten by a teacher may be absolute fiction, but the pain they endured by these figments was very real. For the victim, the dream place becomes a cage to put their demons on display without connecting the emotion to their real tormentors. Some victims wipe the parental abuse out of their memories completely. Others still remember it but attach no emotion to it and can even talk about it freely, almost nonchalantly, "Oh yeah, my dad used to beat the hell out of me every night. Once he broke my arm in three places." Someone listening to this might stare in horror and wonder how this person could be so cavalier in describing such events. It's because the victim has detached himself from those events and attached himself to entirely new ones. The emotion is connected with the fantasy instead of the reality.

Many psychologists believe that most of the people who claim they were abducted by aliens and tortured and molested in hideous ways have transferred some childhood trauma to that fantasy. It's not the most socially acceptable setting, but it is something the victim believes people are unable to refute. How do they know there are no UFOs? In fact, the more legitimacy the subject is given in the media, the more people come forward claiming to have been abductees. Maybe they were. But the psychologists who believe there is a more down-to-earth explanation for these humiliating events usually stress that the victims almost always convince themselves that the fantasy is true, right down to their dreams. The victims even display the shame of their torture when talking about the fantasy. But in the fantasy, the things that happen to the victim are never the victim's fault. Unfortunately many people who were abused as children harbor feelings that the abuse was somehow their fault, something they deserved.

What about Jack's prisoner of war camp? Was it just a way of making a short stint in the army, ending with a discharge, appear more dramatic? Did his tormentors speak Chinese or did they speak Cajun? Did he sneak back and kill the many or only wish he could have killed that one short balding man with the foul temper and the alcohol on his breath? Either it was just another lie, a tall tale, or it was the place where Jack's worst demons lived and continued to beat him, kick him, and torment him for his entire life.

"I believe Jack was telling the truth when he said he was abused by his father as a child," his attorney, Mark White, said. "I also believe that the doctors who diagnosed him with post-traumatic stress disorder made the correct diagnosis—they just made it for the wrong reason."

CHAPTER FOUR

NOT A FAMILY MAN

While Jack was in the army, he married his high school sweetheart, Ruth Hyde. They were married less than two weeks after he was transferred to Fort Hood, Texas, for treatment of his diabetes in April 1952. Jack's one and only child, Jeffrey David Montgomery, was born in November 1953, about ten months after Jack was discharged from the army. When Jeff was born, Jack was back at Southeastern Louisiana, taking a full course of classes, largely in education. For lack of any better ideas, he thought he could become a teacher.

In the fall of 1954, however, Jack packed up his young family and moved from Hammond so he could finish his education in Birmingham, Alabama. On the GI bill, he attended Howard College, which was renamed Samford University years later. There was some thought that Jack would pursue a career in pharmacology, but that petered out quickly, and he continued on toward a degree in education. Tucked away in the woods of a burgeoning suburb just south of Birmingham, Howard College was known for its high academic standards. Jack worked hard at his classes, and he worked hard outside school.

Always fascinated by the electronic media, Jack showed up at the offices of WBRC-TV Channel 6 and asked if there were any jobs available for an eager college student in his mid-twenties who had served time in Korea. They found him a job as a cable boy, a completely unglamorous task. He was responsible for making sure the camera cables and the microphone cords did not get tangled or trip up people in the studio. Jack did the job with enthusiasm, however, and everyone at the TV station took notice of the gregarious young man with the good looks who was always cracking a joke. He was amiable, and everyone liked him. He was just a college student, but he could have worked his way up at the station if he'd wanted to do so.

Jack also got himself a job at the Birmingham Zoo. As he told the story, the job was a reward for a good deed. Supposedly there was a snake loose downtown that had people running this way and that. Jack alone approached the snake and picked it up. Jack said his act was witnessed by the mayor, Jimmy Morgan, and, "He offered me a job at the zoo as the city's first bona fide herpetologist, forty dollars a week. I took it. I was starving." While no one can remember Jack's brave capture of the serpent, no one can quite say that it isn't true. Charles Giorlando, however, worked at the zoo during that time and did not recall Jack to be quite the dragon slayer he years later made himself out to be.

In those days the zoo was essentially one big fenced-in area. Most of the employees were called caretakers, and, like Giorlando, they did whatever needed doing, which included feeding the various animals and cleaning the pens. "There was a crazy old carny that the zoo allowed to stay there in his trailer because he had a big python and a few other snakes. He agreed to keep his snakes on display." The carnival man hired Jack to transfer the snakes from their cages and feed them every day. "What I remember the most is that Jack was scared shitless of the snakes," Giorlando said. "It was pretty funny." Jack didn't last more than a year at the job. A few years later, the old carny was jailed for poisoning the zoo's two bison.

Jack graduated from Howard in the spring of 1957 with a degree in education and took his wife and son back to Louisiana to live in Baton Rouge, about sixty miles west of Hammond. He did a short stint as a city parole officer, but that didn't thrill him. Then Jack put on a coat and tie and walked into the studios of WAIL-AM 1640. He approached the station's morning DJ, Pappy Burge, who was also co-owner of the station, about a job. Burge sent Jack to talk to the other owner, Harold Herthum.

"He was determined and self-confident, but I really don't know why I hired him," Burge said. "He sold airtime—or at least that's what he was supposed to do. He pretty much did as he damn well pleased." Many times Burge spotted Jack's 1957 Chevrolet parked at the Westdale Golf Club. Jack always claimed he was making business connections, but Burge knew better. Once Jack didn't call or show up at the station for a couple of days. When he finally came in, he told Burge he had four flats.

"He was one of those people who always said, 'Oh, I've got something working,' and you'd think, 'Mm, hm. And it's going to snow tomorrow,' " Burge said. He finally let Jack go after almost a year, which, he said, was almost a year longer than he should have let Jack stay at the job. "He was always cocky and determined to be a winner but either didn't realize it took hard work or simply didn't want to do it. More than anything, I think he wanted to become a playboy."

It was obvious that Jack did not want to be a married man with a son, Jack's high school friend Don Sibley said. "He knew some important people and traveled in pretty good company. His clubs, his shoes, his clothes always had to be the finest. But he never acted like he was married. He just didn't seem to want the responsibility of a family."

Frequent golf partner Jesse LaGarde remembered Jack as having "a real good locker room swing. But he was a better dresser than he was a golfer." Still Jack was fun to be around, LaGarde said.

In social situations, people who knew Jack and Ruth realized that something was wrong simply by the way he treated her. "He'd go out of his way to embarrass her in front of everyone, just to make her leave," Sibley said. "I really didn't respect him because of the way he treated his family."

When Jack just up and left his family for good in August 1961, it didn't surprise anyone.

Jack got a job as an advance man for the Bellas Hess chain of discount stores and wound up in Mobile, Alabama, where he supervised the construction of a store in a new shopping center near the airport. Through a friend of a friend, he met Phyllis Ann Laird: twenty-one years old, blond, long-legged, and very attractive. Jack was thirty at the time. Her father owned a marina across from the yacht club, and her parents didn't much approve of the slick older man from Louisiana. Phyllis, however, was thrilled with Jack. He was large, rugged, handsome, a real man's man. He told her he had been in the Green Berets in Korea, and she believed him. But he told her a lot of things. He told her that he was divorced. "Jack was as smooth as smooth could be," Phyllis said. "He could sell you dirty underwear and make you think you were getting a good deal. He was a lot of fun."

Despite the wishes of her parents, Phyllis and Jack continued dating every weekend, going to clubs, dancing, and drinking. It did not take her long, though, to find out that Jack had a deadly serious side in addition to his fun side. "One night, he threw a knife at me," Phyllis said. He was standing on the street by his car, and she was up on the porch of her parents' house. They had been arguing about something silly. Jack was drunk and quite angry. "The knife whizzed right by my head and stuck in the side of the house right next to me. He could have killed me if he had wanted to."

The fright she might have felt at that moment was dulled by the alcohol they consumed that night. She did get the message, though, that Jack was a man of action, capable of anything. To a young woman who had been raised by strict parents but had a wild streak lying just under the surface, Jack seemed like the ticket to excitement. After dating for six months or so, Phyllis ran away from home with Jack, without saying a word to her parents.

Not long before she met Jack, Phyllis had lived for a year or so with friends of her parents in the Philadelphia area, so she and Jack made the trip to Pennsylvania to try their luck up there. Phyllis had done some modeling in Philadelphia and New York, and she figured she could do that again. Jack knew of a cousin of a friend who owned an imported and luxury car dealership up there. Jack got a job selling sports cars, and he and Phyllis decided to get married.

Up until their marriage however, they lived in separate residences. Jack insisted on that. "We waited a while to get married, but I was never really sure what we were waiting on," Phyllis said. "Then one day Jack just said, 'Let's do it.' " Their Delaware County marriage license contained the truth as it suited Jack. He put on the license that he had never been married. He also told the license bureau that he was a real estate developer, even though he was selling cars at the time.

Phyllis did not know it, but Jack had been waiting on his divorce. Ruth had been doing what she could in the East Baton Rouge court. In Louisiana at that time, all she could get at first was a separation. After a year of separation, a divorce could be granted. Attorney Edward Glusman was appointed by the court to represent Jack in his absence. Glusman had the unenviable task of trying to locate Jack and get him to respond to the proceedings. He sent a registered letter and a copy of Ruth's petition for a separation to Jack at an address in Mobile; Jack received and signed for. In the two-paragraph letter, Glusman wrote, "If you have any defense to this suit, please let me hear from you by return mail." He received no answer. Ruth was given a separation on October 24, 1961, a little more than a month after Jack left her. She was given full custody of Jeffrey, who was nearly eight years old.

A year later Ruth, represented by a partner of Glusman's, filed for divorce, on the grounds that they had been separated for a year. A new attorney, Kenneth Scullin, was appointed to represent Jack in his absence, and he too sent a letter to Jack, this time at Philpenn Imported Car Company in Bryn Mawr, Pennsylvania.

In his letter, Scullin wrote, "If you care to contest this matter please forward to me any information which might serve as a defense, as for example that you and your wife have lived as man and wife within the past year. I have no authority to force you to become an actor in this case by filing a separate suit in your name." Scullin received a response in the form of a Western Union telegram sent from Bryn Mawr on November 9, 1962. It said only, "I accept under present terms. Just make it final. John Henry Montgomery Jr."

The divorce was finalized on November 28. Ruth was given full custody of Jeffrey but was not awarded any child support. Nearly seven years later, Ruth sued for and was awarded $100 a month in child support. Up until that time, she said, they had received nothing from Jack, except when he sent Jeffrey $100 for Christmas in 1968. Jeffrey had just turned fifteen.

Six days after his divorce from Ruth, Jack and Phyllis got their marriage license. Three days after that, they were married in a civil ceremony in the small town of Millbourne, Pennsylvania. The ceremony was so forgettable that Phyllis said she doesn't remember anything about it. Phyllis had gotten a job with a funeral company, keeping their books. Thanks to Jack's job, she drove a Cadillac convertible, while Jack drove a Jaguar XKE. He was the top salesman on the lot and enjoyed getting to know the kinds of people who could afford such expensive cars. "He was extremely smart and knew how to play the system," Phyllis said of her husband. "Jack knew how to get whatever he wanted. You know, you can't con a con, and Jack was a con. He was always on to you. He was a fine person, and he loved me with all his heart. I loved him too."

She described their marriage as a series of highs and extreme lows. The lows, she said, usually seemed to involve alcohol and Jack's diabetes. Once, while they still lived in Pennsylvania, she found him on the kitchen floor, crying and acting like he was going to stab himself with a butcher knife. "I did such a good job of talking him out of it that he decided to come at me with the knife," she said. She ran out of the house hollering for the police. When an officer arrived, Jack was himself again and was able to laugh his way out of it, giving the cop a hearty slap on the back as he climbed back into his patrol car and drove off. Once or twice Jack told Phyllis he had been a POW in Korea, but mostly he told her stories of things his father did to him, things like being tied to a tree and being beaten with a leather razor strap.

"Jack just wanted to be loved and accepted. Jack could meet anybody. It was amazing," Phyllis said. At one point, he had made friends with some members of the DuPont family, heirs to the chemical corporation fortune, and they invited Jack and Phyllis to live with them at their estate. "I told Jack that I wasn't about to live with those damn people," Phyllis said. "They gave me the creeps." On weekends, Jack and Phyllis danced and partied, but in Phyllis's estimation Jack was not an alcoholic. He only drank socially, she said. "He just seemed to breeze right through life."

Jack once recalled those days of selling high-priced cars when he said to a reporter, "Oh, it was a wonder to behold. Here's this good old Southern boy playing up to all these Yankee ladies. You know, 'Howdy missy ma'am,' and all." No doubt the Yankee ladies, as many ladies did, found Jack irresistible. Their faces always lit up when this dashing man treated them to the attention and manners he was capable of when really pouring it on. Phyllis never actually caught him with someone, but throughout their short marriage, women were always calling him. That alone was a cause of some of the friction between them.

One day Jack walked up to Phyllis and said he wanted to go to law school. She had never heard him talk about law before that—apparently selling cars did not fulfill his dreams. He always seemed to be holding jobs while dreaming of a career. So far he had considered veterinary medicine and pharmacology, but they didn't work out. Law, he thought, sounded like something he could do well with a little bravado and a lot of bull. "He said he didn't want to go through life being a flunky. 'Well, Jack, if that's what you really want to do, we'll do it,' I told him."

They continued working to save enough money to move and get Jack into law school. In 1964 they headed to Birmingham, Alabama, where Jack had finished his undergraduate work. He figured he could get into Cumberland School of Law, the law school at his alma mater, Howard College. He enrolled that fall but was not a stellar student. He stuck with it, but he thought he could breeze through law school the way he had been breezing through everything else. His grades were not bearing that out. Jack also went back to WBRC–TV Channel 6 and got a weekend job as the on-air announcer, the guy who said, "You're watching WBRC, Channel 6 in Birmingham," during the commercial breaks at the top of each hour. Phyllis got a job at a branch of Jefferson Federal Savings and Loan, and she helped with the books for an exclusive supper club on top of Red Mountain, simply called The Club.

Their marriage came to an abrupt end a year later. Jack's temper was getting worse, and the violence picked up in pace and severity. Phyllis recalled going to work at the bank one day with a black eye. She told everyone that she hit a doorknob, but she was sure no one bought her story. Jack was convinced that Phyllis was cheating on him, but she insisted that she was not. He would fly into rages of jealousy. Then on the night of October 1, 1965, Phyllis woke up to find Jack sitting on the side of the bed with one of his big arms draped over her, mumbling to himself.

When she had gone to bed, he had still been drinking and laughing with a couple of his friends in the other room. Now the friends were gone, and Jack was in one of "those moods." He started telling her that if she just wasn't so damn beautiful, he wouldn't have to worry about her. Then he slapped her several times, grabbed her by the hair, and dragged her into the bathroom. He grabbed his straight razor off of the sink and opened it up. If he cut up her face, he said, she wouldn't be so beautiful anymore. Phyllis jerked away as he swung the razor, and she got out of the bathroom. He caught her at the top of the stairs and pushed her down the long flight. At the bottom of the stairs, she struggled to stand up and started screaming. That caused Jack to back off, and she ran out of the house. At a neighbor's house, she called a girlfriend, who drove over and picked her up.

Phyllis never went back to Jack and filed for divorce two weeks later. She was represented on paper by Attorney Arthur Parker. In reality, she said, Parker represented both of them as a favor to Jack and was able to walk the divorce through the system in a day. In the short testimony included with her bill of complaint, Phyllis said, "On the occasion of our separation, the Respondent [Jack] hit me in the face with his hand and actually hurt me and injured me and threatened my life and I am afraid he will cause serious bodily harm if I continue to live with him."

On paper, Jack represented himself and in a short answer to the complaint waived all rights to testimony and proceedings. He did, however, deny hitting Phyllis. Jack and Phyllis also entered into an equity agreement, in which all furniture and personal property was awarded to Phyllis while their 1963 Pontiac Tempest convertible went to Jack. He also agreed to pay legal fees of $185 to Parker. The divorce was granted on October 15, 1965.

CHAPTER FIVE

ESQUIRE

About a month after Phyllis and Jack divorced, he met Sherrel Williams. Jack had taken a job as the resident manager of a small apartment complex just down the road from his law school. Sherrel was twenty-nine, twice divorced, and the mother of a six-year-old girl, Cynthia.

Sherrel—everyone called her Sherry—had been living in Anaheim, California, and working for a bank. She had just gone through her second divorce, and a girlfriend had begged her to come out and live in California. Sherry had only been there a couple of months and was unhappy. She had left Cynthia back in Alabama, not wanting to transplant her if things didn't work out—and it looked like they weren't going to work out. Sherry came back to Alabama to visit Cynthia and the rest of her relatives in the Birmingham area for a while.

Her brother and his wife lived in the apartments where Jack was the manager. They knew Jack, thought he was a great guy, and set him up with Sherry. "We just kind of clicked," Sherry said. "He was very charming, and he would laugh and cut up. He was like a combination of Robert Goulet and Robert Redford. He had a beautiful smile and piercing blue eyes." Normally Sherry was a no-nonsense, practical person who felt the weight of her responsibilities, but Jack absolutely swept her off her feet. They went to movies and out to dinner. He even cooked for her a few times.

After four weeks of dating, Jack simply said, "You know what? We ought to get married." It took Sherry just a moment to realize he was serious and just a moment more to say she would. They were married on Christmas Eve 1965—Jack's thirty-fifth birthday—at the home of Sherry's sister and her husband in the West End area of Birmingham. The couple stood in front of the Christmas tree and were married by a Methodist minister. Jack wore a dark suit, and Sherry wore a green and tan outfit of suede and wool.

They lived in Jack's apartment for six months until he quit the job as resident manager, and then they moved to a house in Helena, a small town about fifteen miles south of Birmingham, not far from where Sherry was raised. The house belonged to Sherry's sister's mother-in-law, but no one was living in it. Jack was working hard and wasn't home much, doing the weekend announcing at WBRC–TV Channel 6 and going to law school. He was practically failing school when he met Sherry, but it did not take him long to get serious about his grades in an attempt to finally make something of his life. Toward the end of law school, he started clerking for Arthur Parker.

Jack had met Parker at law school and immediately impressed the veteran attorney with his brash, confident nature. He reminded Parker of himself. Parker started his law practice in 1950 and quickly became recognized as one of the most capable criminal defense attorneys in the county. In 1953 he ran unsuccessfully for mayor of Birmingham. Probably the one thing everyone remembered about that campaign was when Parker was supposed to appear on a local television show to discuss his liberal platform of getting blacks on the police force and generally cleaning up what he saw as a corrupt city hall. Before the show, Parker and another attorney, who was supposed to introduce Parker on the show, decided to calm their nerves by going out and grabbing a few drinks. They must have grabbed a few too many because when the attorney stood up to announce the esteemed Mr. Parker on the air, he said, "Ladies and gentlemen, I present to you the next mayor of Birmingham—Arky Parky." Despite his unsuccessful bid for office, Parker kept his hand in local politics, building a base of power behind the scenes.

While Jack was in law school, Sherry got a job working the counter for Delta Airlines. Jack got along fairly well with Sherry's daughter but said he didn't want to be bothered with having any more children. That was fine with Sherry. Jack took Sherry to Louisiana to meet his parents and his son, Jeff.

"His father was a short, balding man. He didn't look anything like Jack," Sherry recalled. "Jack never wanted to stay down there long. He told me his father used to beat him with a bullwhip and do terrible things to him, but I don't know if I ever believed that. By then his father had mellowed out and just seemed like a nice old man." Sherry, though, did believe Jack's story about being a POW in Korea. For the first few years, she had to deal with the nightmares that woke Jack up screaming practically every other night. "It was scary," she said. "I couldn't imagine what they must have done to him."

In law school Jack was known as a loner and not an outstanding student, but he got by. "I remember that Jack reached the conclusion that a lot of the things people fret and fuss over is just horse manure," said classmate Chriss Doss. "He expressed this over and over, and it gave him a kind of carefree attitude because he didn't sweat the small stuff."

In January 1967 Jack got another job, teaching an undergraduate law-related course at Jefferson State Community College in the division of commerce and business administration, mostly because the dean was a friend of his. Jack didn't sweat the small stuff there either. He told the students that if they brought him a fifth of bourbon, he would make sure they did not fail. Sherry remembered that he brought home a lot of bourbon during that time, especially just before finals. That job lasted only a couple of semesters however. A new dean came in, one who didn't care much for Jack, and he did not invite Jack to return.

Jack graduated from law school in the spring of 1967 and went to work full-time for Parker. "Arthur really bragged on Jack," Sherry said. "They were a lot alike, both very confident of their abilities." Jack passed the bar in September and bought a new house in the Center Point area, just northeast of Birmingham. For Sherry, that was the beginning of an ending that lasted another nineteen years.

When Jack became one of the boys, he swelled with self-importance and enjoyed all of the rights and privileges afforded to a white attorney in the Deep South. Jack got busy getting to know people and making them like him. Working for Arthur Parker was a huge stepping-stone, and Jack never missed the opportunity to put his connection to Parker's name to good use. He spent all day practicing at the bar and all night drinking at the bar. He would come home at three or four o'clock in the morning nearly every night, Sherry recalled. "He drank before, but nothing like this," she said. "His bar bills were huge. I bet you could have fed a family for what he was spending at the bars." When he came home, he usually made Sherry's life miserable.

Sherry sent her daughter, who was about ten years old by then, to live with her mother in nearby Alabaster. Her mother had been begging Sherry to let Cynthia live with her, and Sherry saw that as an opportunity to get her young daughter out of a situation that was becoming increasingly volatile. Sherry never knew when Jack was going to fly off the handle about something, and she didn't want Cynthia around when Jack was like that. Alone, Sherry thought she could change Jack.

Arthur Parker did not think much of Jack's legal skills but admitted that the young man had some flair. Jack spent a few years learning at Parker's knee and then went into practice with Attorney Bob Esdale. "I thought he was very good in court," Esdale recalled. "He would talk to the jury with a sense of street smarts, and they always responded to his straightforward approach."

But it was more than that, according to Don Russell, who was a young assistant prosecutor in the district attorney's office and went head-to-head with Jack several times. "Jack was tall and good-looking, and the jury immediately liked him," Russell said. "I always wondered about his knowledge of the law. I think if the law was all he had, he'd have been beaten every time. But Jack played around, always trying to get the jury to like him despite what was going on with the case."

Sometimes Jack wore a special jacket to court on the day of closing arguments. The lining was covered with question marks, and Jack would open his jacket toward the jurors whenever the prosecutor made a key point. The jurors would look at Jack, and he'd sit there with his coat open and shrug as if to say, "What is this guy talking about?" It always got laughs from the jury. The prosecutor would turn and catch Jack, get flustered, and object. The judge always sustained the objections, but the damage had already been done to the prosecutor's case—or at least to the solemn demeanor of his closing argument.

At home Jack suddenly sold his house "right out from under us," Sherry said. "The developer offered Jack a real good deal. We made money, but we had nowhere to go. He was like that. He'd just up and do something, not thinking about how it might affect things." It so happened that Arthur Parker's old house was empty since he had just moved into a larger house he had built. Jack and Sherry moved into Parker's old place and stayed there a couple of months until Jack bought a house in the old part of Vestavia Hills, a bustling suburb just south of Birmingham. The move took Sherry several miles closer to Cynthia. She visited her daughter nearly every weekend, and sometimes Sherry's mother brought Cynthia to their house.

Jack made friends with a couple of judges and managed to get his name put on a list of substitute judges. Years later Jack claimed that a judge had come up to him once and said, "You've got judge blood in you." Certainly Jack came to believe that, and it wasn't long before he started to lust for the prestige of the bench. Getting on the list of substitutes was just a start in that direction. Once he showed everyone that he could do it well, he was certain that a place would be found for him among the brethren.

Parker recalled a case he had before Jack in those early days when Jack was a substitute judge. Parker was representing a man charged with driving under the influence. The arresting officer was on the witness stand, and the prosecutor asked if the defendant had been tested on the Breathalyzer. The officer said he had. The prosecutor asked what level of blood alcohol the machine measured in the defendant.

"Objection, your honor," Parker said. "This officer is not certified to operate and read that machine." The Breathalyzer technician, however, was not in the courtroom.

"No," Jack said with a casual wave of the hand, "I want to hear the answer."

Parker grabbed a book that was sitting in front of him and slammed it down hard on the defense table, giving everyone a start, especially Jack. "Well, then, I quit," Parker said loudly.

"What do you mean?" Jack said. "You can't quit."

"I certainly can," Parker said. "If you're not going to follow the law, then there's no need for me to be here."

Jack hastily called a recess and talked with Parker, who explained the law. Jack then got back on the bench and instructed the prosecution that the evidence from the Breathalyzer could not be entered without the testimony of the certified technician who conducted the test. Since the prosecution could not produce the technician, Jack dismissed the case.

The situation at home was getting worse, and Sherry finally decided to tell Jack that she couldn't live with his drinking, staying out late, and his hair-trigger temper anymore. Jack promised her it would stop soon. The very next night, Sherry got a phone call that Jack was in the hospital. He had been partying at a bar and had fallen down a long flight of stairs. Some of the patrons said he had been pushed by an irate woman. When he hit the bottom, he landed upright, with his weight coming down on his right leg, which was locked. His upper leg bone acted like a pile driver, splintering the top eight inches of the primary bone below his knee into dozens of pieces. Fixing it required a bone graft. Not long after his fall, the bar burned down. Jack delighted in telling people that he had set the fire, but no one believed him.

Between his diabetes and his alcoholism, Jack's recovery was neither short nor simple. He almost died, Sherry said, because the doctors were not sure how to treat him. Years later Jack told people that Sherry saved his life because she had insisted that he be transferred to University Hospital at the University of Alabama at Birmingham. At University Hospital his recovery was more capably handled, and he got better instead of worse. All total, Jack was hospitalized for more than a month, slipping in and out of consciousness most of the time.

One day while Jack was in the first hospital, Sherry was in the room with him when several doctors walked in to get a blood sample. She had told the staff days earlier not to let any Asians into the room since Jack always got agitated because of his time as a prisoner of war in Korea. Still, some of the young doctors purposely invited an unknowing Asian doctor to draw the blood just to see what would happen. "This [Asian] doctor was peering over him, while the others stood back and watched," Sherry said. "I was just hoping that Jack wouldn't wake up." But, Jack's eyes fluttered opened, and he saw the almond-shaped eyes of the young doctor leaning toward him. Jack's right arm, which was tied to a splint and had an intravenous tube in it, jerked up, and his meaty fist landed a punch square in the doctor's face. The blow sent the doctor reeling across the room. Jack didn't say a word—he just fell unconscious again. "The other doctors thought it was funny," Sherry said, "but I was mad."

Another time Sherry was in a waiting room of the hospital when a nurse grabbed her and said, "Thank goodness you're here." She told Sherry that Jack was out of bed and going through a bank of lockers saying that Sherry had been kidnapped by the Chinese army and there were Chinese soldiers hiding in the lockers, waiting to get him. Sherry had to take Jack by the arm, talk him down, and lead him back to bed. "To this day," Sherry said, "I don't know how he could have acted like that if he hadn't been a POW."

After leaving the hospital, Jack spent another month or so on crutches and didn't go back to work. The specialist who treated Jack had told him that if he kept on drinking the way he had been, it would kill him. So the drinking stopped, for a while anyway. Jack's behavior even mellowed a little. He didn't swear as much, and he tried hard to keep his diabetes and his temper in check. He even talked about maybe going to church, but he never did. His temperance lasted almost a year, and he came home early most days. But, Sherry said, the old habits eventually crept back—the only difference was that now he did his drinking at home.

CHAPTER SIX

THE MARLBORO MAN

Jefferson County Criminal Court Judge Burgin Hawkins reached mandatory retirement age in 1974 and had to relinquish his seat on the bench at the end of the year. Thomas E. Huey Jr., the presiding judge of the Tenth Circuit, which included Jefferson County, announced that nominations for the open position would be taken until mid-November. The circuit judges would then meet and elect Hawkins's replacement, as well as a replacement for General Sessions Court Judge Thomas E. Thrift, who also reached mandatory retirement age that year. Nearly forty-four years old, Jack thought he had the judicial experience from being a substitute judge to hold the position full-time, so he entered his name as a candidate. Attorney E. C. Herrin, who had been on his own in general practice for almost ten years and had been acting as a substitute judge like Jack, also entered his name in the race.

Don Russell was in his sixth year as a deputy district attorney, and his competence as a prosecutor had caught the attention of more than a few people. Circuit Court Judge Wallace Gibson asked Russell to place his name in nomination for the open seat. Russell thought about it and decided that being a judge was something he would really like to do. In the days before the circuit judges were to meet and vote, Russell visited each one and took his own poll. "I thought I had it wrapped up," Russell said. "Much more than a majority said they were going to vote for me." Certainly he didn't have anything to worry about from the grandstanding Jack Montgomery. While theatrics were OK for an attorney, they were not suitable for a judge. No, you had to know the law backward and forward to be a judge, and Jack had certainly demonstrated that he did not.

Russell was prosecuting a murder case the day of the vote. University of Alabama running back Bobby Duke Jr., nineteen, had been kidnapped and shot twice with a shotgun in July 1974. Hayes Joseph Tooson, thirty, was caught a few days later driving Duke's car. On the morning of the vote, Russell was set to deliver his closing argument in Tooson's trial. Before he started, though, a friend whispered to him that Robert Vance, who was an official in the local Democratic Party, was in the courthouse visiting all of the circuit judges.

"Well," Russell thought, "that's it. I won't get the judge-ship." For all his legal smarts and ability in the courtroom, Russell was not a political animal. Any fight that came down to politics, he knew he was going to lose. He delivered his summation, and shortly after noon he got word that he had lost by a landslide. Judge Gibson still voted for him, but he was the only one. Jack had won, apparently because Arthur Parker, who by that time carried a lot of clout in the local party, had pulled all the right strings for him. Vance was sent to the court-house to deliver the party's decision. Herrin was having lunch with his wife that day when a circuit judge spotted him and let him know that Jack had been elected. The vote was close, the judge told Herrin.

Jack was not completely unqualified for the bench. He had done well as a substitute, and none of the judges had heard any complaints about him. The added weight of the party's "recommendation" was enough to sway the vote. In the old New South, everyone was a Democrat. Elections were decided on primary day because no one ever voted Republican in the general elections. So when a roomful of Democratic judges, who needed the party's backing the next time they ran for reelection, were given the name of someone the party wanted in the fold, they listened. Now this was not a seat on the supreme court or anything—it was just a county judgeship. Jack was going to handle traffic tickets, bond hearings, and preliminaries. The circuit judges were not going to be that choosy about who they put in that spot.

The same was true for Parker. It was not like he had put his boy in a position of great power—Parker had friends in much higher places. But who knew? Parker believed Jack could do big things, perhaps parlay this position into something bigger. That was the beauty of influence, real long-term influence. You pick a vivacious young man out of a crowd, befriend him, help him through a tough spot, and give him a job. He proves himself worthy, so you boost him up into a small position. From there it's up to him. In a few years, though, you might find your young protégé in a position where he can help you out.

Jack took his oath of office in January 1975. At that time the pay for a county judge had just been raised to $23,180 a year. He wasn't going to get rich, but he did have a title and his own tiny kingdom.

Kathy Hogan, who had been Judge Hawkins's secretary, didn't know anything about her new boss, Jack Montgomery, before he showed up for his first day on the bench. "Most judges were old and dignified. They were always very nice, but kind of plain," she said. "I was surprised when Judge Montgomery walked in for the first time. He was not like the other judges. He was tall with dark hair and so handsome. Ohhh, he looked just like the Marlboro man."

Jack's first official act as a judge was to order a large screen to be placed by Hogan's desk to keep the rabble from bothering her. She was instantly his friend. From the get-go, Jack started to spin his yarns about himself. "He was leaving for the day one time early on," Hogan said, "and I told him it was raining outside. I asked him if he wanted me to get him an umbrella. He said he didn't feel rain because he had been a POW."

It was pretty clear from the start that Jack was not going to be a run-of-the-mill judge. Besides the fact that he looked like the Marlboro man, he continued to be a flashy dresser: plaid sport coats and bright ties. He did not blend into the crowd.

"I liked the way Jack dressed," Sherry said. "It was flamboyant, but he always had style. He shopped for his own clothes, and he would have the linings of his jackets custom-made. He had one that was zebra stripes inside. His clothes matched him—sharp."

Charles Arndt was Jack's tailor for many years. The two first met in Mobile, where Arndt was the manager of a clothing store and Jack was working construction. Arndt moved to Birmingham and opened his own tailoring shop. One day he saw Jack walking down the street and pulled his old customer into his new shop.

"He didn't dress like other lawyers or judges," Arndt said. "He liked bright colors, and he always knew which colors went well together. He was the kind of customer who always knew what he wanted. The linings of his jackets were usually bright designs or paisleys."

After Jack became a judge, he decided it was time to have a jacket made with a lining that had the word "Guilty" stitched all over it. Many a defendant trying to talk his way out of a criminal charge in those early days watched Jack slowly raise his large frame up above the bench and open both sides of his jacket wide to reveal his cloak of "guilt." Just as when he was a lawyer, the trick always got snickers from the people in the courtroom, but now Jack could get away with it—no one could tell him not to pull stunts like that.

Jack refused to wear a judicial robe. Whenever the media would ask him why, he'd say something about how it got in his way or made it tough on his bum leg. In private, however, his response was always, "Anyone who needs to wear a black dress to prove that he's a judge isn't really fit to be a judge."

That comment, which was one of his favorites, actually said a lot about Jack. Tossing aside any possible he-man phobia about wearing dresses, it spoke of Jack's feelings of inadequacy that plagued him his whole time on the bench. Jack knew that his command of the law was only fair, and he knew that as jurists many judges were his superiors. But he had to be the center of attention, the best in the room. He looked down his nose at most judges in order to prop up his own self-esteem. They were too caught up in technicalities, he would say. They weren't interested in getting to the heart of the matter, only in being proper and correct. And most lawyers believed that Jack had a ton of horse sense, which was sometimes necessary in district court. Still he never felt quite like a member of the club. For Jack there were two options: Struggle to join the club or assume that you're too good for them. Jack chose the latter. By not wearing a robe, Jack gave himself the opportunity to show that he was different, and to him different was definitely better, even if he did not truly feel that he was better.

Jack was one of those people, his wives said, who felt deep down that he was a fraud. The one thing that frightened him the most was that other people would find out he was fraud. So he never allowed anyone to get too close to him. Jack made himself so big, so bad, and so bold that hopefully no one would figure out the truth. It was the "heaping bullshit" theory: If you heaped enough bullshit on something, people would just get tired of digging. Jack quickly got a reputation for being a blustery, foul-mouthed judge, the likes of which no one had really seen before. This was the South, where ceremony and courtesy were highly regarded, and this guy was like a wet polecat with a gavel. And the lawyers never knew when he might start messing with their cases, questioning witnesses himself, or passing unusual sentences.

Jack did not try to fly his courtroom entirely by the seat of his pants however. "He was very excited about being a judge," Sherry said. "He knew as soon as he got it that this was the position he was looking for. He loved the attention, and he loved being able to tell people what to do. He worked hard to keep up with decisions and new laws, and it worried him that he might miss something. He hated for lawyers to correct him or show him up in the courtroom." He was quite serious about his job, and he took it as something of a mission. Jack felt he was the perfect person to straighten out other people's messes, to issue the proclamations from on high. He just didn't want all of that silly law crap getting in the way.

During the first few years Jack was on the bench, things between him and Sherry remained fairly uneventful. They moved to another house in the suburb of Vestavia Hills, this one in a more exclusive section on Rocky Ridge Road. The rambling ranch house sat well back on a steep hill, with a large shady yard. "Jack liked it because it was secluded, and he put a fence around the yard to make it even more secluded," Sherry said. He busied himself making changes to the house, enlarging the bedroom and redoing the kitchen. And he had a swimming pool built beside the house.

But Jack also started drinking more. Because he was a judge, he almost never went out to drink. Instead he would sit in front of the TV and pour down the bourbon. Sherry never really knew what to expect when she got home from the job she still had with Delta. Between the diabetes and the alcohol, there was a fifty-fifty chance Jack would be in a foul mood. "It truly was like living with Dr. Jekyll and Mr. Hyde," she said. And there was always the chance that things would be exceptionally bad. Cynthia still lived with Sherry's mother, but she sometimes called Jack. They had forged something of a friendship, and when Jack was in a good mood, the teenage girl enjoyed talking to him. Sometimes she came by the house just to see Jack.

One night Sherry had stopped at the grocery store on her way home. When she walked into the house, she saw Jack sitting in a chair with a glower on his face that told her right away things were exceptionally bad. Realizing that his blood-sugar level was too low, she tried to get him to drink a Coke. He wouldn't, and he was adamant about it. Figuring that she should just leave him alone, she walked down the hallway. He followed her.

When they got to the bedroom door, Jack pushed her in. Then he shoved her onto the bed and climbed on top of her. He started choking her with one hand, and then he drew back the other as if he were about to punch her tiny face with his big, heavy fist.

"Don't do this, Jack," she said as calmly as she could. "If you hit me, you know you'll be in serious trouble. The police will find out, and they'll arrest you."

Her words broke through the fog momentarily. He grunted, lowered his fist, and let go of her neck. Then he got up and went into the bathroom. Sherry quietly slipped off of the bed and walked out of the door, her legs shaking from the fear and adrenaline. He could have killed her. She knew that. She got in her car and just drove around town for a few hours.

Jack also knew that he was capable of murder that night. He managed to arouse himself from his hypoglycemia enough to realize that Sherry was gone, and he remembered that he had harmed her. He picked up the phone and dialed Sherry's sister in Trussville.

"I think I killed Sherry," he said. "She's not here. I must have taken her out into the woods and killed her. I'm sorry. I don't know why I did it."

Sherry stopped on the road and called her family from a pay phone shortly after Jack called and told them she was fine and would be staying with them for the night. They had been panic-stricken for a few moments. The next morning Sherry went home to Jack, and he was relieved to see her. "He was always apologetic afterward," she said. "It was difficult to be mad at him because he was ill. It was the diabetes that was doing this to him. Still, it took its toll on me."

Whenever Jack got into one of his spells, Sherry simply tried to stay as far away from him as possible. When that was not possible, she did not fight back. "I knew he would really hurt me if I did that."

Jack kept up with his insulin shots, but he did not eat regularly, and the drinking played havoc with his diabetes. "Sometimes he could be the most lovable, concerned person you can imagine," she said. He often put her on a pedestal and made her feel like the most important person in the world. One time he came by the Delta office and gave her a diamond-and-emerald ring for no particular reason. He didn't even have anything to apologize for at the time. "Then there were times when he was just so angry. He was never angry about anything important, just angry."

One time while Jack and Sherry were at home, he suffered terrible chest pains. Sherry took Jack to the hospital, thinking he had suffered a heart attack. The doctors detected a slightly irregular beat and some other problems. The specialist called Sherry into his office and told her that Jack had suffered a heart attack and that they were going to do an arteriogram. Depending on what the test showed, the doctor said, open-heart surgery might be a very real possibility.

The arteriogram showed that Jack had not had a heart attack—but he did suffer from an irregular heartbeat. The doctors kept Jack overnight and said they wanted to perform more tests. The next morning Jack called Sherry and told her to come pick him up. He had checked himself out of the cardio-intensive care unit. "He was like that," Sherry said. "He just refused to take care of himself. I asked him to stay in the hospital and let the doctors check him out more, but he refused."

Although she never saw him in action in his courtroom and Jack never talked about his cases, Sherry knew he was showing his true colors in court too. Once while she was working at the Delta ticket counter in a downtown hotel, one of the other local judges came in to buy some tickets. When the judge recognized Sherry from the couple of social functions she and Jack had actually attended, he asked her, "How can you stand to live with him? He's crazy."

It was getting so that Jack didn't have to be drunk or hypoglycemic to be nasty to Sherry. Once his son, Jeff, brought his wife up to Birmingham from Louisiana to attend the football game between the University of Alabama and Louisiana State University at Birmingham's Legion Field. They called Jack and said they wanted to get together with him and Sherry, so the four of them met for dinner at a restaurant. Jack and Jeff had been talking awhile, and Sherry and Jeff's wife were having a separate conversation, as so often happens at the dinner table. Suddenly Jack turned to Sherry with fire in his eyes and said, "Would you just shut your damn mouth?" Sherry was mortified and didn't speak for the rest of the dinner.

When she and Jack got in the car after dinner, she looked at him stonily and said, "Don't you ever in public tell me to shut up again."

Jack looked sheepish and said, "You're right. I'm sorry."

She knew that he was sorry. She also knew that being sorry wasn't going to prevent him from doing it again.

In his more lucid moments, with some incident of Jack's behavior still fresh in their minds, Sherry would suggest to Jack that he seek psychiatric help. "He didn't want any part of it," she recalled. "He didn't think that would help him. That's what seemed so sad to me. He could've gotten help, but he chose not to."

In 1980 Sherry finally decided she'd had enough of Jack's foul language and foul moods. Her mother had taken ill. Sherry used that as an excuse to move out of their house and in with her mother. She and Jack continued to talk to each other on the phone, and she came home every once in a while. Jack usually stayed quiet while she was home, not wanting to do anything wrong. A couple of times Sherry was tempted to move back in with him, but she caught herself in time to realize that things would eventually go back to the way they had been.

"I never thought Jack went out on me," Sherry said, "even for most of the time we were separated. He flirted a lot, but I just never got the impression that he was unfaithful."

Jack insisted Sherry accompany him when he went out socially, especially to official dinners and parties with other judges. He was very big on keeping up the appearance that they were still together. Every so often Sherry mentioned divorce, but Jack cried and pleaded for her not to do it. "Why get divorced?" he would ask. "What would change? It's just a piece of paper."

During that time Sherry's daughter, Cynthia, continued to have contact with Jack, especially when she was in trouble. In her late teens and early twenties, Cynthia had some problems, not the least of which was alcohol, according to Sherry. One night Cynthia had a car accident while intoxicated. She was not seriously hurt, but she was disoriented. She left her car behind and stumbled to Jack's house, which was not far away. She crawled in through the doggie door, and Jack found her on his kitchen floor. He cleaned her up, took care of her, and handled the details of cleaning up the accident.

"I was glad that she trusted him and that he cared enough to help her," Sherry said. "They kept up their friendship for a long time."

For six years Jack and Sherry kept up appearances and stayed married until Sherry finally demanded a divorce. It was right after Jack's mother died, and she knew the timing was hard on him, but she needed to move on. Sherry remarried soon after and left Birmingham.

"It wasn't all bad," she said. "We had periods of being happy and periods of being unhappy. Deep inside Jack was a good person, but he was troubled."

CHAPTER SEVEN

A STAR IS BORN

Tom York was an institution in Birmingham television. It's a cliché, but no other term fits. He was that one guy you find in every city who started in local TV when local TV only reached five or six homes and then decided to stick around for a few decades. He wasn't especially good-looking, and he certainly wasn't tall. But York had a smooth, pleasant voice, professional but still trustworthy. Toward the end of his career, young broadcasters were being hired who were more attractive and more poised. York, though, lent continuity to a market where on-air personalities came and went just as soon as someone in a bigger market saw their tapes. He had staying power because he stayed. He knew the station and the market inside and out. He was never a big celebrity, but folks just got used to seeing him on the tube, day after day, year after year. The old folks loved him.

He started in radio, as almost all of the early TV personalities did, while he was going to Florence State Teachers College. Later he moved into TV at a station in Memphis, where he was director of public affairs and read the sports. WBRC–TV Channel 6 in Birmingham hired him in 1957, making him the staff announcer and the sports director. In those early days of local TV, everybody at a station usually did two or three things, so York also hosted the *Dialing for Dollars* program and was the pitchman on a lot of local commercials. When he heard there was an open slot in the schedule between seven and eight o'clock on weekday mornings and the head office was trying to figure out how to fill it, York volunteered to do a show. And so *The Tom York Morning Show* was born.

"We did it live, of course," York recalled. "Even after videotape became commonplace, we still did everything live. I was the first in morning television to do exercises, long before aerobics. We had a medical show every Thursday, and we had brokerage people talk about investments. We were winging it most of the time, but it was a good show."

York had his share of performing dogs and cooking segments and kindergarten teachers too. Like York, the show had staying power, and it was the only source of local programming in Birmingham outside the newscasts. That's what viewers and even nonviewers seemed to appreciate the most about York's show. At least, they would say, there was one show in Birmingham that was about Birmingham. Individually few daily broadcasts were that memorable. As a body of work the show was part of the city.

Around 1980 Jack called York. They knew each other from Jack's days as a college student and a law school student working at Channel 6 more than twenty years earlier. In fact it was York who had hired Jack to be the weekend announcer. On the phone, Jack said it was election time and he needed to bolster his image. He asked York if he could use a judge for his show to talk about the criminal justice system on a regular basis. York said it sounded like a great idea. He knew something about Jack's reputation as a judge, and he remembered the college student as a gregarious young man who was comfortable with the idea of being on the air.

The first few shows with Jack produced some uneventful interviews. Jack kept himself in check and tried to act like a judge, blandly answering technical questions about the law— they were fairly forgettable segments. York basically told the judge that if he really wanted to make an impression, he should let loose, be himself. He opened Pandora's box with that advice.

Jack quickly became one of the show's most popular guests, appearing twice a month when he could. He peppered his comments with "hells" and "damns" that tended to shake viewers out of their morning fogs, and he talked about the law as if he was just an average guy who happened to be on the inside. To keep things spicy, York decided to refer to Jack on the air as the "Slamming Judge." He couldn't really say the "Hanging Judge," so he borrowed a term from another popular form of TV, professional wrestling.

People ate it up. They had never heard a judge talk like that before. Jack shattered the image people had of judges as reserved, boring old men who had no idea of what life in the real world was like. It made a star out of Jack, and that was fine with him. "He talked a language people wanted to hear," York said. "He cut out a lot of the bullshit, and he put the fear of God into the street criminals."

And he entertained a lot of kids. As they sat in front of their kitchen TVs, kids all over central Alabama crunched on their cereal before school while watching this crazy guy who was supposed to be a judge. Even they realized that Jack was outlandish, and they thought he was funny. Some of those kids appeared in Jack's courtroom years later as young police officers or lawyers.

Birmingham magazine, a publication sponsored by the chamber of commerce, printed a story about Jack with the headline "The Show Biz Judge," establishing Jack as not just another guy in a black dress. In that article Jack was quoted as saying, "I guess I have become a sort of local celebrity. Yeah, I know I have, because everywhere I go, I'm recognized. Sure, I like it for a lot of reasons. Number one, I am a ham, OK? I like having people come up to me and ask me to answer questions. Besides, I'm back in show biz." Most of all Jack loved people to ask him questions so he could give smart-ass answers and make everyone in the room laugh.

"I can single-handedly reach more people in fifteen minutes than all the rest of the people around," Jack said in defense of his TV stint. "So I'm using this as a vehicle to disperse information to quell the feeling that the courthouse is only for the rich and all. You see, it's an information ladle for me. I can spoon it out."

When people looked in their bowls, though, they saw nothing but Jack. He never saw his appearances on the show as a vehicle for goodwill or education. He saw it as a vehicle for himself, a way to further build his reputation and make it more possible to rub elbows with impressive people. "Jack was posturing, and I loved it," York said. "He came across as being bigger than life. Sure he was using me, but that was OK with me because I was using him."

York always felt a little bit like a lion tamer when Jack was with him live on the air. York had a whip and a chair, and it was understood that he was in charge. But he also knew that if the lion decided he was going to take a bite out of York's leg, there wasn't a thing in the world he could do about it. "I always worried that some inappropriate language was going to slip out," York said, "or that he would say something so shocking it would be a big embarrassment." After discussing some legal issue for a few minutes, they usually took a couple of phone calls from viewers who had questions for Jack. Once a viewer asked the judge about personal protection. To demonstrate his answer, Jack pulled out his own weapon. York just watched helplessly, wondering how many station or FCC rules and regulations they were breaking.

Jack once appeared on the show wearing a T-shirt with the Shakespearean quote about killing all the lawyers. At times it was practically like a vaudeville act, with York playing the straight man. "You like putting people in jail, don't you?" York once asked.

"I really do," Jack said. "I've wanted to do it ever since I was born."

"What do you think of defense attorneys?"

"They're all right if you cook them properly."

"What is the status of the prison population?"

"Well, it's going up, thank God."

One viewer called the show and asked Jack why he didn't run for a higher office. The judge replied that was the first time anyone suggested he run for anything besides the county line.

"Sometimes people would call and just give him hell," York recalled. "I think he liked those calls the best. He could make a joke and have that person laughing in a minute." York himself would bait Jack if things were getting a little slow. As the host, he loved that he could just wind up the judge and watch him go.

Back at the courthouse, the other judges usually smiled when they saw this picture of the hanging judge on TV. "He wanted to appear very macho to the public," said John Bryan, who was the presiding circuit judge at that time. "We'd joke a little, saying, 'Yes, sir, the world needs more judges like Jack Montgomery.' But I thought some of the things he said on the air were better left unsaid by a judge. I didn't call him on the carpet about it, but I finally told him that I didn't think his appearances were appropriate."

Jack believed the other judges had become jealous of his popularity because they simply didn't have the guts to get on the air and tell it like it was. He may have been right. They knew he was not a top-shelf judge, yet he was becoming the best-known judge in the area. Others, though, felt that while they could do nothing about Jack's behavior in his courtroom, they could do something about the way he made all of them look on TV. They could pressure him to stop. So he agreed to put a stop to it. Besides, he had gotten what he wanted out of it. After more than two years on the air, Jack was bigger than life all over central Alabama, not just in the county courthouse.

Five years later York called it quits when he saw that he was about to lose control of his own show. The TV station brought in new hosts, but the show simply limped along for a few more years. Tom York was *The Morning Show*. People had watched because York was an old friend. When York said good-bye, many of them did too.

"Jack had a great need for attention and recognition," York said. "He was onstage all of the time. I never set foot in his courtroom, but after seeing him on the show so much, I think I had a pretty clear picture of what he was like as a judge: profane but concerned, serious but silly. I liked Jack. I didn't have to approve of him to like him."

CHAPTER EIGHT

JACK'S DANCE

Any attorney who spent time in Jack Montgomery's court-room usually had a big decision to make: how to deal with Jack. The judge seemed to delight in making lawyers scramble. He screamed at them, he flung folders at them, he interfered with the questioning of their witnesses, and he sometimes dared them to do what they thought was right. Many people have said that Jack was a bully, and there was no one he bullied more than lawyers. In 1979 Don Russell was appointed assistant district attorney in Jack's courtroom, which was still called county court at that time. His assignment was to clean up the prosecutor's end of things down there.

"It was incredible," Russell recalled about his arrival in the huge courtroom. "The place was packed, and the hallway was full of people. It took me a year and a half to get our cases all caught up and have some kind of working system."

Above it all, Jack reigned. All of the chaos and disorder in the room was constantly reflected in his demeanor. "It was like God created Jack for misdemeanor court," Russell said. "He had a knack for taking these arguments between neighbors or family members and digging out the truth. Sooner or later he'd accuse one of the people involved of something, and he'd be right, and you'd think, 'Damn, how did he figure that out?' "

But Jack's skill often came at a price. "You just had to know how to handle him," Russell said. "The old guys like me, we knew what Jack was about. He was usually playing a game. He tried to make you mad. He was full of bullshit. He'd holler and holler just because he was bored. One time he called me a chickenshit motherfucker. I just nodded and said, 'Yes, Judge.' "

He called lawyers "hebes" if they were Jewish, "wops" if they were Italian, and so on. He did not use the "n-word" in court, but he wasn't shy about using it in small groups.

The experienced lawyers, if they thought Jack had done something legally out of line, could ask to see him in his chambers. More often than not, if they cited the law at question and a few cases, Jack would say, "Yeah, I understand. I don't want to do it, but I'll do it." They'd go back into the courtroom, and Jack would do whatever the lawyer had been asking for.

When Laura Petro was assigned from the district attorney's office to Jack's courtroom, she quickly learned that if she was going to survive, she had to take it with a smile and sometimes dish it back out. Because her father was Lebanese, Jack sometimes referred to Petro as a "dune coon." He often swatted her on the behind when he walked by her. When speaking directly to her, he often called her "DA babe." She simply responded by saying, "Yes, judge babe?"

Petro remembered once taking a newly hired female assistant district attorney around the courthouse to meet judges and other key personnel. When Petro introduced the young woman to Jack, the first words out of his mouth were, "Show me your tits." The woman did not comply.

Average people who were in his court for the first time, often to contest traffic tickets, were appalled at his behavior, Petro said. Those who were familiar with it, though, usually shrugged and said, "That's just Jack."

"He hated preliminary hearings," Petro said. "He tried to intimidate defense attorneys into waiving them." She recalled one attorney, who was defending a man on a rape charge, insisting on a preliminary hearing. The hearing was scheduled, and the victim was put on the witness stand. Petro had only asked the woman her name when Jack, as he often did, jumped in.

"Did that man over there do something to you?" he asked.

"Yes," she said. "He raped me."

Jack brought his gavel down with a whap and bound the case over to grand jury and raised the defendant's bond. "You wanted a preliminary hearing? By God, I gave you a preliminary hearing," he said to the defense attorney.

One earnest young defense attorney came into the courtroom talking about constitutional rights and demanding a preliminary hearing. Petro offered the lawyer a lower misdemeanor charge for his client, but the attorney still insisted on the hearing. After the hearing started, Jack stopped the proceeding and asked Petro if she had offered the defense a misdemeanor in this case. When she said she had, Jack "hit the roof," she recalled. "I tried to warn the guy. Jack just chewed him up. I don't think I ever saw him in that courtroom again."

Petro had been on the receiving end too. Her first case in Jack's court was a murder case. She had no sooner opened her mouth when he started yelling at her and dismissed the case. She was in shock and thought she'd lose her job for sure. When she told Russell, he just laughed and welcomed her to Jack's court.

Scott Boudreaux was still wet behind the ears and working his second day in the district attorney's office when he was sent down to handle the preliminary hearings for the day in Jack's court. He was in the courtroom, looking through his files, when he heard a voice boom, "Hey, asshole." Boudreaux looked up and realized it was Jack addressing him. Apparently Jack had learned that a young Tulane graduate was in his courtroom. Being a Louisiana State University fan, Jack decided the Tulane grad was in need of some derision. "I figured out after a while that was just his way of doing things," Boudreaux said. "You almost took it as kind of a compliment to have him call you names or yell at you. Better to be an asshole than not be noticed at all."

As a prosecutor and later as a defense attorney, Boudreaux learned that timing was everything in Jack's courtroom. "You had to know when to stand up and when to sit down and shut up," he said. One day in Jack's courtroom Boudreaux saw a Mexican defendant who did not speak much English. Apparently it was pick-on-Mexicans day, and Jack was delighting in jerking the migrant worker around a little. Seeing that the poor man did not have any representation, Boudreaux stepped up and volunteered to represent him if for no other reason than to prevent Jack from locking him away somewhere on a DUI charge. That, certainly, may have been Jack's plan all along since no one had been asking for the job until that point.

When Judge John Bryan was the presiding circuit judge, he received plenty of complaints about Jack's behavior in the courtroom. "I called him in several times about his temperament and demeanor," Bryan said. "When he was abusive to a lawyer, I probably made allowances because I heard he had been a POW. He never attempted to justify his actions, he'd simply accept his reprimand. He could be as charming as anyone, but he could be very crude too." There were judges, especially circuit judges, who avoided Jack around the courthouse, in the lunchroom, and in the rare social situation, Bryan said, because they were simply afraid he would say or do something offensive.

There was a short list of defense attorneys Jack did not mess with—he always treated them with respect and deference. Arthur Parker, of course, sat at the top of that list.

Richard Jaffee, one of the more high-profile young defense attorneys in Birmingham, could not even look at the list. He started his career trolling for cases in Jack's courtroom. He was one of those Jack picked on often because Jaffee wouldn't take much of the judge's guff. He did not usually think Jack was funny, and he didn't like being one of the boys. Back in those cattle-call days when the lawyers were looking for cases, Jack would do things like line them all up and tell the defendant, "Pick one of these lawyers. Don't want to? OK, I'll pick one." Because Jaffee was Jewish, Jack would often say, "Naw, Jaffee, this man wants a good Christian lawyer," or he'd say, "Who needs a good Jew lawyer?"

"A lot of the time he was just kidding," Jaffee said. "He was a comedian using whoever he could, like he was Don Rickles. He picked at us for everyone else's amusement." If a young lawyer did not know what he or she was doing, Jack would rip them up one side and down the other. A few he even brought to tears.

"If I had been in there as a young lawyer," Russell said, "I imagine he would have intimidated the hell out of me. If he thought he could bully you, he'd bully you right out of the door. But if you laughed at him, maintained your composure, and maybe even stood up to him when it was important, you were fine."

As Jaffee gained experience and some stature, however, it stopped being just fun and games for him. "He didn't like me, and he told me that in open court and in private. That didn't bother me. What bothered me was that Jack would trample the rights of my clients because he didn't like me."

Once Jaffee insisted on a preliminary hearing for the Birmingham police officer he was representing. Jack flat refused. "He was screaming at me. He became an animal. His face was beet red, and he was practically foaming at the mouth." A bailiff was pleading with Jaffee to stop. Jack threatened to throw Jaffee in jail if he kept insisting, but Jaffee wouldn't let up. He finally got the preliminary hearing for his client, and the officer was later acquitted of the charges against her.

With defendants Jack could be kind, harsh, or uncaring—depending on the circumstances or Jack's mood that day. If a defendant was down on his or her luck and seemed sincere, Jack had been known to be moved to the point of giving them some cash out of his own pocket. Contrition was important to Jack. The rare criminal who appeared truly sorry for doing wrong usually found some forgiveness in Jack's court. Most defendants, though, were treated with a heavy hand. Jack got so testy with defendants who didn't seem capable of answering the few simple questions he was required to ask them that his bailiffs sometimes used cue cards. "Has your attorney discussed these charges with you?" Jack would ask.

"Yes, sir," the defendant would read off the cue card.

"Do you have anything you wish to add at this time?" the judge would ask.

"No, sir," the defendant would read off the other card.

When accepting pleas or setting bond, knowing a defendant would be out on the street within a couple of hours, Jack did what the law could not—he scared them. He often addressed a defendant as "Hoss," and he would point a big finger at him and look him right in the eyes. "If they bring you back in here, Hoss," he would say, "I'm going to make you sorry your mother ever brought you into this world. You got me?"

At first the defendant would hang his head and mumble, "Yeah."

"What's that, Hoss?" Jack would say so loudly that everyone looked up.

The defendant's head would snap back up, eyes wide. "Yes, sir."

And then Jack would give the defendant a look, one that said he would make good on his threat if he had to. After a moment, he'd say, "Now get out of here." The defendant would nearly run out of the courtroom.

With witnesses, especially in sensitive cases like rape or child molestation, Jack was more unpredictable. He could bring witnesses to tears, to the point that they swore they would never testify again. Or he could sit on the floor and coax a child to testify to the court in more detail than even the pro-secutor had heard to that point.

"For the most part," Jaffee said, "I think he was the kind of person who could understand the frailty of human beings. That's rare in a judge."

CHAPTER NINE

JACK'S BEST FRIEND

Steve Anderton stood before Judge Jack Montgomery in September 1979 after being found guilty. Jack gave Anderton the harshest penalty he could: three months in jail plus a $500 fine and court costs.

That may not sound like much, but the charge was a misdemeanor—cruelty to animals. Jack, disgusted with Anderton throughout the hearing, said he wished he could do more to punish the young man. A neighbor of Anderton's testified that she heard puppies crying one day and went to a nearby field to find out what was wrong. She came across a large piece of plywood, and the puppy sounds seemed to be coming from under it. When she lifted the plywood, she saw one black puppy trying to crawl out. Three others were burned and dead. She picked up the one that was still alive and noticed that his underside was burned. "I held him up against my cheek to comfort him," she said. "That's when I smelled the gasoline."

Anderton's little brother, Chris, said Steve's dog had seven pups and that his brother was planning to drown the puppies that had long tails. Jefferson County's animal cruelty officer, Deputy Bill Carter, testified that the puppies had been doused with gasoline and burned alive. Two were burned beyond recognition, and the third was badly singed. Defense attorney Carl Chamblee asked Carter if the humane society didn't also kill animals, as many as 40,000 dogs a year.

Jack stopped Chamblee right there. "How many animals the humane society has to kill is not relevant to this case," the judge said, "unless you are telling me they pour gasoline on them and set them afire." Chamblee admitted that was not his point.

Anderton could not have asked for a worse judge to hear his case. If there was one thing Jack could not abide, it was cruelty to animals. When Jack was through with him, Anderton was glad the judge was limited in the severity of the sentence he could give him. Ever since he was a kid, Jack had been an animal lover. When he was in high school, he was elected president of the Junior Wildlife Club, an organization of more than 200 boys. As an adult, his affection focused on dogs. But like everyone or everything else Jack loved, even dogs could try his patience, and they occasionally felt the brunt of his irrational temper.

When Jack and Phyllis were in New Orleans for a short trip, Phyllis bought a purebred tricolor basset hound and named him Hoover, "like a vacuum cleaner," she said. "If it fell on the floor, he got it." Three days after she got him, she found out from a vet that Hoover suffered from a form of distemper. She babied him and cooked him a liver dinner every night. Jack was fond of the dog, but once, in one of his moods, he threw a can of shaving cream at Hoover and hit him in the middle of his back, leaving a permanent lump. After Jack and Phyllis moved to Birmingham, Phyllis bought a female red-and-white basset and named her Missy. The night Jack pushed Phyllis down the steps, he pushed Missy with her. When Phyllis left, she took the dogs with her.

Sherry gave Jack a Doberman as a present when he graduated from law school. "He said he wanted a Doberman because they looked stately and threatening," Sherry said. "I found a woman who raised Dobermans and went out to her place and bought the pick of the litter." She was planning to leave the puppy with her mother until Jack graduated. When the dog's papers were delivered to their house though, Jack saw them and wanted the dog right then. He named it Nemo and loved that dog as much as he could love anything. Nemo was very attuned to his master and did just what he wanted. He would sometimes bark at Sherry but never at Jack.

Jack taught Nemo to act viciously toward strangers, but he was actually a gentle dog. Police officers who came to Jack's house refused to come inside when they saw Nemo baring his teeth. Once Jack had a hypoglycemic attack at the house and called the fire department. When the paramedics arrived, Jack had passed out and Nemo stood between his master and the strangers, daring them to come closer. The paramedics had to spray Nemo with a fire extinguisher to get to Jack. The dog was like Jack's guns—it added to his reputation as a tough guy, and he loved that.

Sherry later got a springer spaniel and named it Kouklara. Actually the full name was Ise Kouklara Mou, which is Greek for "you are my pretty girl," and Jack and Sherry took to calling her Prissy. Then Jack bought another Doberman, a trained dog that had already been named Satan. The dogs had the run of the house. They had a doggie door and their own queen-size bed in the bedroom. Jack fed them from the table. He loved all of them, but not like he loved Nemo. When Nemo died of heartworms after twelve years, Jack had him cremated and kept the ashes in a small gold box.

Prissy, it turned out, had a somewhat nasty temperment that Jack and Sherry had not counted on. Don Russell remembered one day when Jack came to the courthouse looking pale. "We sat him down and asked him what happened," Russell said. "On the one hand I couldn't believe the story he told us, but on the other hand it sounded like vintage Jack."

Jack told them that he had been cutting his grass on his riding lawnmower and daydreaming about daredevil motor-cyclists and how they jump over cars and buses and how that looked like fun. When he spied a small ridge in the yard and the rosebush on the other side, he bet himself that if he could get up enough speed on the lawnmower while going over that ridge, he could probably clear the rosebush. Sure enough, he got over the bush, but the lawnmower flipped over when it hit the ground, and it threw Jack. He got stuck under the fence, and Prissy got so agitated that she chewed up Jack's left arm. Russell and one of Jack's bailiffs convinced Jack to go see a doctor about his arm.

Jack took all of his dogs to Riverview Animal Clinic in nearby Shelby County, and Dr. Arthur Serwitz usually took care of them himself. One day an employee of the clinic called Serwitz to the front lobby. Jack, who was all red in the face, had just brought Prissy in and yelled at the girl, "I want you to put this goddamn dog to sleep!" Then he turned and walked out, leaving Prissy behind.

Serwitz ran out into the parking lot and caught up with Jack. He put his hand on the judge's shoulder and said, "You don't want to put that dog to sleep."

Jack stopped and slumped forward. "Yeah, I know," he said wearily. "Just keep it for a few days, will you? I'll be back to get it."

Serwitz didn't know what had happened, but the dog had obviously done something to make Jack mad. Prissy chewed on Jack several times, usually when he had gotten into a hypoglycemic spell and was feeling ornery himself. Still, he cared for Prissy, who suffered from epilepsy, and he always kept the house quite cold because she did not have much tolerance for heat.

After Satan died, Jack and his fourth wife, Jennifer, bought a purebred boxer and named him Toby. They even attended some meetings of the local boxer club. But when that marriage went awry, Jack gave Toby to the guy who trimmed his trees.

In July 1987 a stray, injured Doberman made the right choice when he wandered into the judges' parking lot of the Jefferson

County Courthouse. From a window in the courthouse, Jack spotted a couple of construction workers talking to the dog. Something was obviously wrong with it. Jack went downstairs and approached the red Doberman. "He was real tired, as if he'd been up a long time," Jack said later. "I said, 'Hey, what's your name?' and he didn't answer. Without having a response, I looked at the dog and saw that he was dirty and bleeding. There was a good chunk taken out of his hip." Jack walked toward the back door of the courthouse, turned to the dog, and said, "Come on, let's go." The dog stood and followed Jack into the courthouse.

The two made an odd sight parading through the halls of justice, past the lawyers and bailiffs, Judge Jack Montgomery with this weary, bloodied Doberman obediently trailing behind, his nails clicking on the granite floors. Once in Jack's chambers, the dog loped onto the couch and curled up. Jack asked the dog a couple more questions. "He took the Fifth Amendment," Jack said of his new friend. He offered the dog some water, but he wasn't interested. He started calling the dog C. J., for Criminal Justice, loaded C. J. into his car, and drove him to Riverview Clinic. Dr. Serwitz examined the dog and found that he was suffering from heartworms, an ear infection, and a wound on his right hip. After Nick Patterson wrote a story about the dog for the *Birmingham Post-Herald*, Serwitz got a number of calls from people saying they wanted to adopt C. J. The dog was given to one of those people, and in November of that year, Jack was given the Birmingham Humane Society's Brodnax Award for saving C. J.

One Christmas, Birmingham photographer Spider Martin got a phone call from Jack. Spider had photographed the judge for the *Birmingham* magazine story, and he knew him as most people did as a tough, foul-mouthed SOB. But he liked the crusty old judge and affectionately called him "Wild Man." The newspapers had just printed a full-page public service advertisement for the Nash Frank Society that was built around a picture Spider had taken of an adorable, pathetic little puppy in a cage. Jack told Spider that when he saw that ad, he went back into his chambers, locked the door, and cried like a baby. "I realize now that I'm a human being," Jack told him. "That's the best Christmas present I ever got."

CHAPTER TEN

A COLOSSAL SLIP
OF THE PEN

Jack Montgomery ran a tight ship in his courtroom, but every once in a great while someone got away with murder. The judge never had a good explanation for it, and it seemed to depend on who the killer had for a lawyer.

Take the case of Clinton J. "Joe" Kelley. His wife, Barbara "Bobbie" Harris Kelley, forty, was shot to death in their modest house in Gardendale, a town just north of Birmingham, on May 21, 1980. The police took Joe, sixty-two, into custody that night and charged him with murder a few days later. Mrs. Kelley was a part-time nurse at the Gardendale Nursing Home, and she and her husband had been arguing. Their sixteen-year-old son was at the neighbor's when Mrs. Kelley came running out of the house with a rifle in her hand. Joe came out after her, they went back into the house, and then there were three gunshots. Mrs. Kelley had been shot three times in the head with a .38-caliber pistol.

Joe Kelley was represented by attorney Jesse Shotts, one of Jack's law school pals. In fact Shotts was about as close to Jack as it was possible to get. Years later he was one of the few lawyers Jack put on his list of substitute judges. Before anyone really knew what happened, Jack accepted a plea of manslaughter from Kelley and sentenced him to ten years in prison, which was suspended to five years on probation. Not a bad deal—shoot your spouse in the head three times and get five years probation. Of course this was not an ambush or a carefully planned murder, it was a crime of passion, committed in the heat of an argument, and Mrs. Kelley had been armed. Joe was not going to do life in prison no matter what. Still, three times in the head indicated a certain amount of overkill.

The sentence shocked the police officers involved in the case, who did not find out about it until a few days later. They called *Birmingham Post-Herald* reporter Jane Aldridge, who called Jack. During that interview, Jane asked him why he had accepted a plea of manslaughter instead of the murder charge that had been filed against Kelley. Jack replied that if, in fact, the papers said "manslaughter," then "I made a colossal slip of the pen. What I intended to write was 'murder.' " It is fascinating that such a mistake would benefit the client of a close friend.

Shotts, of course, told Aldridge that he was surprised the sentence was so stiff. "Frankly, we expected something better than ten years and five years probation when we entered the open plea," Shotts said. "I think if we'd actually gone to trial, it was a case we could well have won."

An "open" plea is one that the judge accepts without any input from the prosecutor's office. Chief Deputy District Attorney Claude Vines, who was in charge of the Kelley case, said his office was not notified of the plea or sentence until after it was all over. "It was a closed-door deal," Vines said. "We'll never know how it was arranged. Jack was a loose cannon—you never knew what he was going to do, and this was definitely one of those times. Had we been consulted, we never would have agreed to that arrangement. Our office had a big push on at that time not to accept probation in plea agreements, especially in murder cases."

Despite what Jack claimed was a mistake, he never went back and changed the "manslaughter" notation on the record. And prosecutors had no recourse. Defendants can appeal sentences, but prosecutors can't. Later Mrs. Kelley's family sued Joe for wrongful death and won $75,000. He tried his best to hide his assets from them, signing over his property to relatives. When contacted at his home in Florida years later, Joe Kelley denied that anything unusual happened between his lawyer and Jack. "Besides," he said, "I didn't kill that damn woman."

Then there was the shooting death of twenty-year-old Richard Bryant out by West Jefferson Lake on the afternoon of Sunday, July 12, 1987. Richard had gone to the lake with his sister Teresa, his girlfriend Donna Carr, and his friend Terry Phillips. Teresa said the four of them were standing around talking when two cars drove up and four young men they had never seen before got out. "They started smart-mouthing us and then started talking nasty to me," she recalled. "Richard was taking up for me and telling them not to talk to me like that." Richard got into a fistfight with one of them. Two more of the young men jumped on Richard before Teresa came to his aid. "Before long the attackers said, 'OK, just let us leave—let us leave' " Teresa said. They got back into their cars, but one of the cars wouldn't start. "Richard did something to their battery so they could start it. Can you believe that? He fixed their car."

That, of course, was Teresa's story. Investigators later said that one of the men pulled a gun on Richard, and Richard pulled out a tire iron. He hit the guy who had the gun and then broke some windows out of one of their cars with the tire iron.

After the young men left, Richard and his group left too. But Terry realized he had lost his wallet, so they turned around and went back to look for it. When they got back, they saw three of the young men from earlier standing near the top of a hill. "They were yelling, 'We're going to kill you. We're going to kill you,' " Teresa said. "So I went up the hill and said, 'Why can't we just be friends?' But they kept saying, 'We want your brother. We're going to kill him.' " She started back down the hill but then heard five or six gunshots. They sounded like firecrackers.

Richard was standing next to his girlfriend Donna at the bottom of the hill. He asked her for a cigarette, and "then I saw blood squirting out of his neck," she said. "He walked about four feet to the car and fell down. He tried to say something, but all he could do was look up." The coroner's office said Richard had been shot in the left side of the neck with a small caliber weapon from about 150 feet and the bullet had lodged in his lung.

Sergeant Tom Swatek of the Jefferson County Sheriff's office was assigned to the case, and he soon arrested Nickey Charles Freeman, twenty-six, along with three other young men and charged them with murder. Swatek believed the evidence showed that Freeman was the shooter. Freeman retained Arthur Parker as his attorney, the same Arthur Parker who gave Jack his start in law and practically put him on the bench. And Freeman was scheduled for a preliminary hearing in Jack's court. On the morning of the hearing, Jack called Swatek into his chambers. "He told me, 'You don't have a damn thing here,' when he knew as well as I did that I had eyewitnesses and evidence, including a weapon," Swatek said. "He said he wanted to dismiss the case, and I told him to his face that he was crazy."

Freeman and his lawyer never did show up for the hearing, and later that day, Jack entered Freeman's guilty plea to criminally negligent homicide as well as a sentence of one year's probation. The deputy district attorney on the case, Mike Anderton, said Jack did it all on his own and over Anderton's objections. Swatek felt like he'd been mugged in the county courthouse. "That's the best case I ever saw go right down the tubes," Swatek said. "Jack Montgomery was a bully, and he'd been dirty for years. He may not have always done it for money, but he sure did it for his friends."

One of the other defendants in the case, Kenneth Wayne Townley, was sentenced to ten years in prison for his role in Richard Bryant's death after pleading guilty to manslaughter before a different judge. Another defendant, Burl Wayne Marlin, got five years' probation after also pleading guilty to manslaughter before a different judge. Charges against the fourth man were dropped.

Freeman, by the way, broke Jack's short probation when he tossed a hand grenade at a policeman in the small Jefferson County town of Graysville. The officer, Eddie Jones, wasn't hurt in the blast, but he sure was surprised to find out that it was Freeman who tossed the grenade at him. "We thought he was supposed to be in prison on a murder case. The last we had heard, they had him cold on that murder at the lake. We were all kind of puzzled as to why he wasn't locked up somewhere. I put the blame right on Jack Montgomery for nearly getting me killed." Freeman received a ten-year sentence in federal court for the hand grenade.

Arthur Parker, of course, had a different take on the murder case. "The reason this thing was settled was the fact that he wasn't guilty and the evidence was circumstantial and weak," he said. "My conscience hurt me for taking the plea because I thought I could win the case outright. I was never convinced that Nickey Freeman did that. I would say that, yes, Jack's actions were unusual, but it was a crappy case." Parker did, however, admit that he had more influence with Jack than most lawyers did. "And when dealing in the law, influence can be an important aspect. I assure you, though, that if Jack did anything because he thought he was doing me a favor, it was not because I specifically asked him to."

No one in the Birmingham legal community has ever said anything about Parker except that he was beyond reproach, the dean of lawyers. But no one has denied the profound effect he had on Jack's career. Parker continued his practice right up until his death in 1995.

CHAPTER ELEVEN

GUNPLAY

Everyone knew that Judge Jack Montgomery carried at least one gun with him at all times, even into the courtroom. He made sure they knew. And if they forgot, he'd pull it out every once in a while and let everyone get a good look at it. Don Russell was in Jack's courtroom once when he noticed the judge look up as a man walked in and sat down in the back of the room. Don had never seen the guy before, but Jack just kept staring at him and the guy kept eyeballing Jack right back.

All of a sudden Jack jumped up from the bench and rushed out into the gallery where the man was sitting. Jack pulled out his pistol, stuck it in the guy's face, and hollered, "I don't know who you are, but you don't walk into my courtroom and act like you own the place." The guy looked down, and Jack holstered his weapon, walked back to the bench, and sat down. The guy got up and left.

"I never said a word about that to Jack, never asked him about it," Russell said. "To be honest, I don't know if they set that up as a gag, or if it was really what it looked like it was."

The guns were a big part of the macho image for Jack. He was not a hunter and didn't like people who did hunt. He could never kill an animal but always claimed he could kill a person if he had to. Of course he also claimed that he had killed people before. Aside from the macho image, guns gave a feeling of security and self-importance to a guy who ran high on paranoia and low on self-esteem. If someone were gunning for him, and he was sure that someone usually was, he refused to be caught without a way to fight back. And he was sure that he could always have the last word if he wanted it. He once told a reporter who was writing a profile of him, "I'd rather have a gun and not need it than need a gun and not have one. If you come up to my front side and say you're gonna kill me, you'd better have your gun in your hand before I have mine in your mouth. I can take care of myself."

Once in court Jack was actually presented with a valid opportunity to shoot someone, but for all his talk, he proved to be slow on the draw. Thirty-one-year-old Gary Landers Hargrove, who was charged with breaking and entering was a defendant in district court in June 1982. A short preliminary hearing was held before Jack's colleague, Judge W. W. "Red" Stewart, and Hargrove's case was bound over to the grand jury. At the beginning of the hearing, Hargrove refused to turn around in his chair to face the judge. His attorney finally convinced him to turn around. That was the only indication he gave that he might cause trouble.

When the hearing ended and Bailiff Larry Ross walked by, Hargrove lunged at Ross and grabbed his gun, even though his hands were cuffed. With both hands on the butt of the gun, Hargrove tried to pull it up and out of Ross's holster. Ross clamped his hands over Hargrove's hands and pushed down, struggling to keep the gun in his holster. For one adrenaline-filled moment, everything stopped except the two men locked in their life and death struggle. Judge Stewart ducked under his desk. He had seen Jack just a moment earlier standing in the back doorway to the courtroom—he had simply stopped by to bullshit with the folks in Stewart's court. Jack later told reporters that when the struggle for the gun began, he pulled out his own gun. Stewart said he never saw that, mostly because he was ducking for cover.

It was Bailiff Chris Galbaugh, though, who pulled out his own .357 Magnum and shot Hargrove in the gut. Hargrove fell with a thud but survived the wound to go to prison another day. "I damn sure would have shot him too, if I'd had the chance," Jack was quoted as saying. "I'm a witness and almost executioner."

But Stewart wondered how Jack could have even thought of shooting. "I'm glad he didn't," Stewart said. "The bench was between him and where the defendant was. If he had shot, he would have shot me."

Nobody had any problem with what Galbaugh did, including Hargrove's court-appointed attorney, Robert Ison. "In my opinion, it was justifiable," Ison said. "If he had gotten the gun, there's no telling what he would have done with it."

Jack, too, stood behind the bailiff's actions. "Suppose the man had gotten the gun out of the holster and shot six people?" he said. "That's a chance you can't take."

While having a gun at his side gave Jack confidence, it sometimes made the people around him more than a little uncomfortable. Bailiff Mac Parsons learned that guns and diabetics susceptible to hypoglycemia really don't mix. Parsons had failed to recognize the signs of low blood sugar one day until it was too late. Sheriff's Deputy Dennis Blanton had done something that ticked off Jack. The judge responded by pulling out his gun, pointing it at Blanton, and screaming, "Get out of my courtroom or I'll blow your damn head off!" Blanton left the courtroom, leaving Parsons to deal with the judge. The only thing he could think of was to get that gun away from Jack.

He approached the judge and told him he had just gotten a phone call from the jail and that there was a situation that required Jack's personal attention immediately. The two of them walked to the jail, where even judges and police officers had to relinquish their weapons before entering. "I got the first gun off him without a problem," Parsons recalled, "but he wouldn't give up the second one. He was kind of waving it around and saying stuff that didn't make much sense." Parsons kept telling Jack that he couldn't go inside unless he put all his guns in the secure drawer. When he finally got the judge to release the gun, Parsons's intention was to take Jack to the jail cafeteria for some orange juice to raise his blood-sugar level.

A warden had witnessed Jack's actions at the gun drawer, however, and assumed Jack was drunk and belligerent. The warden had two deputies take Jack and Parsons to a jail cell, where they were both locked in until Jack cooled down and the jail officers could figure out what was going on. Instead, it just made things worse. "Jack was raving and screaming like a maniac," Parsons said. "I just didn't know what to do at that point."

There was another prisoner in the cell with them. He looked at Parsons and asked, "What's wrong with him?" Parsons explained that Jack was diabetic, his blood-sugar level was too low, and he needed something with sugar in it. The prisoner nodded, leaned forward, and said slightly louder, "Hey, Judge, I've got a pear here you can have."

Jack whirled around and took a step or two toward the prisoner and yelled, "I'll shove that pear up your ass, and then I'll charge you with trying to bribe me with a pear!" Then he turned back around and returned to yelling obscenities through the jail bars. Eventually he tired out a bit, and Parsons and a couple of deputies led him to the cafeteria. They got some orange juice into Jack, and he just went limp. The next day in court, Parsons couldn't help but wince when he saw that Jack had his pistols back.

As a reporter who had covered the courts for the *Birmingham Post-Herald* for several years, Nick Patterson was well acquainted with the fact that Jack always had a gun within arm's reach, but he'd never gotten a close-up look. One day he walked into the courtroom to ask the judge a question for a story he was writing. When he told Bailiff Chris Galbaugh he was looking for Jack, Galbaugh replied that the judge was in his chambers. "But you don't want to go in there now, Nick," he said. Patterson, though, insisted that he had to ask Jack about something. Galbaugh said the judge was awfully upset about the cartoon that had appeared in the *Post-Herald* that morning. The editorial cartoon, drawn by Walt Guthrie, showed Jack dressed as a clown. Patterson waved off Galbaugh's warning, saying he didn't have anything to do with the cartoon and the judge knew that.

When Patterson entered the outer office of Jack's chambers, he saw a couple of lawyers inside with Jack, so he waited by the window. A few minutes later Jack walked out of his office, and Patterson got his attention. "Hi, Judge. I've got a question for you." Jack turned and started walking toward Patterson. As he did, he pulled out one of his pistols and drew it to bear in Patterson's direction.

"Nick," he said, "you're lucky that I know you didn't have anything to do with that cartoon." He cocked the gun and pointed it at the windowsill right next to Patterson.

"You know I didn't, Judge," Patterson said.

"Yeah, I know. Otherwise I'd blow your black ass away."

Jack put away his gun and smiled. Patterson stammered out his question, and the judge responded with something unremarkable and left. Patterson wandered out into the hallway and stopped for a moment. He realized he never felt seriously threatened, but he was still shaking a little. If one little muscle had cramped in Jack's hand at the wrong time, Patterson thought, the paramedics would be reaching him right about now. Patterson mulled over the incident for a couple of days but didn't tell anyone. Finally an attorney stopped him in a hallway and asked, "What's this I hear about Jack Montgomery pulling his gun on you?" Patterson shrugged it off but decided he had better tell the editor of the *Post-Herald* what had happened. The editor decided he would at least make a call to the Judicial Inquiry Commission and ask if pointing weapons at reporters was proper behavior for a judge.

A week or so later Patterson ran into Jack, and the judge said, "Hey, we're cool, right? Of course we are," and that was that. Patterson still respected the judge and, for the most part, found his court antics amusing. But after that incident, he also knew the judge could go a little too far.

There was one instance in which someone threatened Jack with his own gun, and he didn't seem to like it one little bit. It was a warm day in early April, and Charles Arndt's clothing store was busy with businessmen shopping for spring suits on their lunch breaks. Jack strode into the shop and saw that all of the employees were busy with other customers—none of them even acknowledged his presence. Jack stood there for a minute, being ignored, and then he decided that was enough. He started yelling and screaming in the middle of the store that he was Arndt's oldest and most important customer. He screamed obscenities at the staff and customers and pretty much carried on like a madman. After every customer had hurried out of the store, Jack stopped shouting, let out a little grunt, turned around, and left the store too. Arndt was fuming—not only had Jack chased out all the customers, but he didn't even buy anything himself.

The next day the scenario was the same—a warm day and the shop was busy with lunchtime customers. Arndt looked up in time to see Jack through the window, heading for the store. Arndt asked the customer he was helping to excuse him for a second, and he headed for the door, where he met Jack. This next part comes under the heading "Your tailor knows things about you that no one else does." Arndt locked his eyes onto Jack's as he sidled up to him. Deftly, without so much as looking down, Arndt reached under Jack's jacket and put his hand around the butt of Jack's pistol—he knew exactly where he wore it. "If you come in here and pitch another scene and chase my customers away like you did yesterday," Arndt hissed under his breath, "I will squeeze the trigger of this gun and blow your you-know-what off."

Arndt removed his hand and took a step back to allow Jack into the shop. Instead, without a word, Jack turned around and left. He never went back to Arndt's shop after that.

CHAPTER TWELVE

TALL TALES

Judge Jack Montgomery stood at the podium before the Hoover Chamber of Commerce in May 1982. He was the lunch speaker, the day's entertainment, and he intended to be entertaining. He told them that all murderers should be publicly executed. "Strap that sucker in the chair and fry his butt. But do you get to see it? No. Does that make sense—killing him after all that expense and hiding it? It's got to be done at halftime at the Super Bowl."

This was Jack's element, putting on a show for folks he had never met before. In reality he certainly didn't treat all those charged with murder in such harsh terms, but he liked for people to think he did. He was larger than life, and a figure as big as he was needed big stories.

Everybody had a favorite Jack story. A few of them were simply part of the courthouse vernacular, legends that everyone knew. Some of them really happened, and others he simply made up. At least one of the psychologists who examined Jack in the last years of his life said the judge had a penchant for creating self-aggrandizing exaggerations. People who worked with him said you didn't need a degree in psychology to come to that conclusion. Jack was fond of telling people, especially when his racism was questioned, "Hell, I used to be black." He would get quizzical looks and then laugh and explain that his daddy was Cajun, and back in the 1930s Cajuns were considered to be nonwhite.

So under "Race" on his birth certificate, the word "colored" was supplied. He also said he had that designation changed in the 1970s. There is no evidence, however, to support his story.

Jack told the enthralled members of the Hoover Chamber of Commerce that he was presiding over a hearing (actually, he said trial, but he didn't preside over trials) on a rape charge. "It looked like the husband of the rape victim was so mad that he was going to haul off and shoot the defendant right there in the courtroom," Jack recounted. "Well, I saw I would be in the line of fire if he did. I said, 'Oh, God, if he misses him, he's going to hit me.' So I called the husband to the bench and said, 'What's this, Hoss, are you going to shoot him?' And he said, 'Oh no, Judge, I'm gonna stab him.' I said, 'Oh, that's all right.' "

The businessmen laughed long and lustily at Jack's story. Did it happen? Who knows. But Jack was damn sure every one of those people was going to go back to work and repeat that story at least once.

Several attorneys talk about the times when Jack pulled out a quarter and watched the defendant's eyes get as big as saucers when he explained that he was going to flip the coin. "Heads, you get probation; tails, I send you to prison. OK?" he'd tell the poor slob. He'd flip it, and they'd nearly collapse with relief when Jack looked at his hand and said, "Heads. It must be your lucky day, son." He never did what the coin told him to do, but he loved the effect it had on the defendants.

Jack got national media attention in 1984 when he sentenced a man to six months in jail and a $1,000 fine for touching a woman. The man said in court that he touched the woman, whom he didn't know, while they were in the Laundromat because he couldn't resist her tight jeans (the woman later testified that her jeans weren't even that tight). At the Laundromat the guy had gotten into a wrestling match with the woman's husband, who was trying to prevent him from leaving before the police arrived. The media seemed to think Jack's penalty was a bit harsh. When one newscaster asked him what he would have done if the case had been turned around and a woman had touched a man, Jack said that "under the law it would have been the same. Men and women don't like to have themselves touched by people—complete strangers, or sometimes friends for that matter." Yet Jack was the judge who smacked female lawyers on the rump.

A particular defendant, in the midst of his preliminary hearing, stood up and clutched his chest. He made some choking noises, gasped for air, and then dropped to the floor. Several people crowded around him, loosened his shirt, and tried to make him comfortable. One of the bailiffs called the fire department, and when the paramedics arrived, they hooked him up to the heart monitor. Jack stood a couple of feet away without saying a word. When the monitor was functioning, the paramedics noted that the man's heart was beating normally. Jack swooped in and bent over the defendant until his face was just a couple of inches away. "You're not having a fucking heart attack," Jack yelled at him. "If you don't die, I'm going to kill you myself. Now stand up." The guy stood up and brushed himself off, looking a bit sheepish. The hearing continued.

Jack's attacks of hypoglycemia were not faked, however, and they were of great concern to lawyers who had to be in his courtroom—they also became part of the legend. Many times people in the courthouse whispered to each other about how Jack had passed out in the hall or the cafeteria. Every once in a while, one could catch wind of another police officer finding Jack's car pulled off the side of the road with Jack unconscious inside.

"You really had to feel sorry for him," Don Russell said. "It wasn't unusual to see Jack slumping against the wall, having trouble walking. We'd do what we could for him when he got that way. Usually a Coke would bring him around, and then he'd go on like nothing had happened."

Probably the most often repeated story, and surely Jack's favorite, had also been verified by court personnel. The judge got word that a defendant in the lockup had threatened Jack's life. Jack told a bailiff to bring the guy up to his fifth-floor courtroom. The man was brought to him, and Jack said, "I hear you want to kill me. Here's your chance."

"What can I do?" the man asked. "I'm in handcuffs."

Jack told the bailiff to take off the handcuffs. With only one hand free, the man threatened to jump out of the window.

Jack said, "Wait a minute. Do you mind if we open the window first? Oh, and can we get those handcuffs back? I hate to have a perfectly good pair of cuffs ruined when you go splat on the sidewalk."

The man just looked at Jack for a moment. Then he turned to the bailiff and said, "Put these cuffs back on me. That man's crazy."

Jack liked to call people's bluffs. Once he was handling a case that involved someone who was hearing impaired. That person was on the stand, and there was an interpreter in the court for the testimony. Jack noticed someone in the gallery who was also hearing impaired and saying something with sign language in the direction of the witness. The judge asked the interpreter what that person in the gallery was saying. The interpreter replied that the person had just threatened to kill Jack.

"Excuse me for just a minute," Jack said, and he got up from the bench and walked into the gallery and up to the guy who threatened him. The judge started screaming at the man until veins were popping up on his neck. "You want to kill me?" he screamed. "Start it. Go ahead—start something." Even though the guy didn't hear a word of it, he started crying.

Those confrontations were nothing compared to the ones Jack wished he had and tried to pass off as the truth. Sam Tenenbaum Jr., a local professional wrestler who wore a mask and went by the name the "Great Kaiser," once met Jack in a bar and recalled clearly an unbelievable story the judge told him. "I remember a guy I sentenced on a rape charge," Jack told the Great Kaiser between drinks. "He told me, 'When I get out, I'm going to get you.' When he got out on parole, he called me from Texas. I said, 'Where are you, you sumbitch?' He said he was in Houston. I said, 'I'm going down there to meet you.' I went down there and found him in a Laundromat. I beat the crap out of him. Put him in a coma. He died in the hospital." Jack said he wasn't about to wait around for the guy to come get him.

"Jack told me that if he hadn't been a judge, he probably would have been a wrestler," Tenenbaum said. "You know what? I think he would have been a very good one. They could have called him The Judge."

CHAPTER THIRTEEN

THE FORTY-FOOT GORILLA

In Alabama all judges are elected. Yes, the electoral process does seem to fly in the face of maintaining judicial objectivity. After all how can a judge always rule the way he sees fit when he knows that he needs the lawyers he rules against to fund his next campaign? More important, how can a judge be expected to make the correct yet largely unpopular decision in a case knowing that he has to win votes to stay in office? For those reasons and more, nearly every justice organization in the country has for years been calling for the abolishment of judicial elections. But the folks in Alabama are loath to give up their long-standing traditions. It's too simple to think of Southerners as backward or even evil, as in the case of their fight for slavery. Folks in the South are generally comfortable with their lives and comfortable with each other. Men call women darlin' even if they just met. Waitresses call their customers sweetheart. It's just the neighborly thing to do.

If someone takes offense at these terms of endearment, Southerners immediately think the person must be from up North. Then they think that the person is strung a little too tight. Southerners consider the Deep South to be the friendliest place on earth—if you just get on their wavelength. That is not to say that there isn't plenty of flat-out ignorant thinking in the South, but folks are just as reluctant to give up what some see as their evil ways as they are to give up their friendly ways. And woe unto the person who tries to change things—witness the carpetbaggers of the 1890s and the Freedom Riders of the 1960s.

So take away Alabamians' right to vote for the local judge? Not a chance. Not in this lifetime. That's the way things have always been done. They're comfortable with it. Would it have lasted this long if it wasn't the right thing to do? Of course not.

While Jack was initially placed on the bench by appointment to replace a retired judge, he had to run for reelection every six years. Those must have been fiery campaigns, full of allegations and counterallegations. Surely Jack, of all people, could not have run a clean campaign. He must have made the usual mudslingers look like schoolmarms—just imagine.

Well imagination is all there is to rely on because Jack never did campaign for reelection. In the four times Jack had to run for the six-year-long term, no one ever chose to run against him. He always filed campaign funds disclosure forms with the Alabama Secretary of State's office, as he was required by law, and all of them read "0"—he never raised a dime in campaign funds. Jack's absolute favorite quote for the press was "I love this job. I'd fight a forty-foot gorilla for this job and beat him to death. I was born to be a judge." People took Jack at his word about that. Actually it probably would have been a pretty good fight.

Potential opponents were afraid of him personally, and they were afraid of him politically. "Run against Jack?" one attorney said. "You'd have to be crazier than he was to run against him, and nobody was that crazy." Jack's frequent television appearances and outspoken ways made him highly popular with just plain folks who had no idea what actually happened in the courthouse. He was only a district judge, but he was probably the best-known judge in the county. Folks thought Jack was tough, he talked common sense, and he didn't seem like the kind of judge who would turn criminals loose on some stupid technicality.

Politically, Jack was that forty-foot gorilla, and he could sit anywhere he wanted. Why then didn't he set his sights higher? Why didn't he run for circuit court or even the court of criminal appeals? Because he could never have gotten away with what he did in district court. At the district court level, almost nothing was conducted for the record so there were never any transcripts. In circuit court, whenever he called a lawyer a Jew or a woman a bitch, it would have been taken down by a court reporter. Plus, circuit judges' decisions could be appealed, and when they are overturned, the appeals judges issue written statements telling the lower court judges what they did wrong and what they should have done. Sure, when a district judge sets bond, that can be appealed to another district judge or a circuit judge, but who cares? The amount was changed and that was that. As for the other functions of a district judge, it was unheard of to appeal a decision to be bound over to a grand jury or to accept a plea bargain.

Jack was able to be the way he was and do the things he did because he sat at the bottom of the judicial food chain. He was king of the catfish and mudskippers, and that was the way he liked it. Besides, anything higher was too much work. Circuit judges held trials. Jack didn't even like preliminary hearings, and they were cakewalks compared to full-blown jury trials—no way could a circuit judge fly through the docket and then go home after lunch every day. The higher up the ladder it went, the more complicated and time-consuming it all got.

This is not to say that he did not worry at election time. "He was deathly afraid that someone would file as a candidate," Sherry said. "He put himself through the wringer every time. You know, he was just so paranoid. I don't know what he would have done if he'd had to run against someone."

In reality many incumbent judges do not face opposition. Lawyers aren't usually eager to put their careers on the line by running against a judge and losing and then facing that judge in the courtroom again. When Sandra Ross Storm filed against Circuit Judge Charles Nice, Jack told her she had "balls made out of brass." She still chuckles over that one. Nice was the family court judge who had been under heavy criticism because he refused to let juvenile defendants be tried on capital offenses, regardless of what they did. When Ross won, Jack said he was going to have some brass balls mounted on a plaque for her. He never did, but her race against Nice certainly must have reinforced his fear of having to run for his office.

In the 1986 preelection period, Jack tweaked his tactics a little when he had a bumper sticker printed and put one on the car he drove to the courthouse. The sticker read "File against me and die."

Jack Montgomery as a self-confident attorney

Jack's second wife, Sherrel, once said that Jack "was very charming, and he would laugh and cut up. He was like a combination of Robert Goulet and Robert Redford. He had a beautiful smile and piercing blue eyes."

Jack Montgomery showing off his custom-made "question mark" jacket

During closing arguments Jack would sit facing the jury, and whenever the prosecutor made a key point, Jack would open his question mark-lined coat and shrug as if to say, "What is this guy talking about?" It always got laughs from the jury and flustered objections from the prosecutor. The judge invariably sustained the objections, but the damage had already been done.

Jack Montgomery (left) and James C. Manning (center) being sworn in by Judge Thomas E. Huey Jr. (January 1975)

Jack as a no-nonsense judge

When accepting pleas or setting bond and knowing defendants would be out on the street within a couple of hours, Jack did what the law could not—he scared them. Pointing a big finger at each defendant and looking him straight in the eyes, he would say, "If they bring you back in here, Hoss, I'm going to make you sorry your mother ever brought you into this world. You got me?"

The day this cartoon ran in the *Birmingham Post-Herald,* Jack happened to see reporter Nick Patterson in the courthouse. Jack pulled out one of his pistols, pointed it at Nick, and said, "Nick, you're lucky that I know you didn't have anything to do with that cartoon." Then Jack cocked the gun and pointed it at the windowsill next to Nick. "You know I didn't, Judge," Nick said. "Yeah, I know. Otherwise I'd blow your black ass away," Jack replied, smiling and tucking his gun back under his jacket.

Photograph by Kendra Sawyer

Hoover Police Sergeant Mark Hobbs

Mark Hobbs made the state attorney's case against Jack Montgomery possible. With his chiseled, All-American face, Hobbs looked like the kind of guy who, when he showed up on the front porch to pick up a date, any dad would slip ten bucks into his hand for a pizza after the movie. The fact that he could conduct undercover drug investigations with a face that should be on milk commercials may have been Hobbs's greatest feat.

FBI Special Agent Steve Brannan

Assistant U.S. Attorney Bob McGregor made the right decision the night two nervous Hoover police officers, Mark Hobbs and partner Ray Chaffin, came to his house to talk about Jack Montgomery's racketeering. He called FBI Special Agent Steve Brannan. If anybody knew how to catch a crooked judge, Brannan did. "Steve was a damn good agent," McGregor said. "I was impressed with his work on other cases, and this one was going to take finesse and patience."

FBI surveillance photographs of bail bondsman Warren King *(top)* meeting with an informant in front of the Jefferson County Courthouse (October 6, 1992) and *(bottom)* undercover agent Terry Fisher leaving Warren King's residence (October 22, 1992)

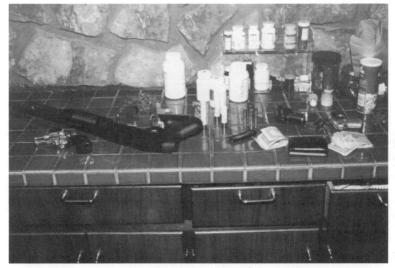

When FBI agents executed a search warrant at Jack Montgomery's
house the night of October 22, 1993, they found a variety of guns,
Jack's prescription medications, and the marked money used in
the bribery sting.

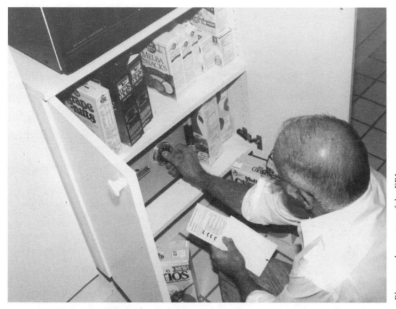

(Top) Jack Montgomery agreed to open the safe at his house for FBI agents the night of October 22, 1993. *(Bottom)* The safe held several stacks of cash, some of it marked money used in the bribery sting.

Attorney Mark White

Despite the things his client and longtime friend Jack Montgomery
had apparently done, Mark White defended Jack with everything
he had. White was prepared to make the government prove its case
against Jack, but Jack eventually opted for a plea. Asked by a reporter
if he was worried about Jack's health or what he might do to himself,
White said simply, "I worry about him every day."

Photograph by Kendra Sawyer

U.S. District Judge Sharon Lovelace Blackburn

For those who knew Jack, it may have been the ultimate irony
that his case was assigned to Judge Sharon Lovelace Blackburn.
Jack had not only drawn a woman, which almost certainly galled
him, but he had drawn the first woman to serve on a federal bench
in Alabama.

Photograph by Kendra Sawyer

Assistant U.S. Attorney Mike Rasmussen

Jack's case had been assigned from the start to Mike Rasmussen, a tireless, no-nonsense prosecutor whose calm demeanor and capacity for detail were perfectly suited to the rigid requirements of federal court and specifically to the mind-numbing thoroughness demanded in public corruption cases.

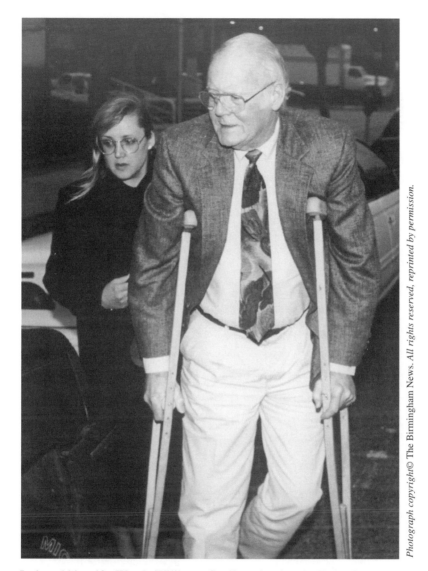

Jack and his wife, Wendy Williams, finally arrived at the Federal Courthouse in Birmingham for his day in court. His broken hip still healing, Jack used crutches to get around. Instead of jury selection, however, the day was filled with closed-door meetings, and a rumor started that there was a plea in the air.

Courtesy of Walt Guthrie

For most people the mystery of Jack's death, like the enigma of his life, has become the subject of good sport. And like all good legends, Jack's story has continued to enjoy life long after the man himself enjoyed life.

CHAPTER FOURTEEN

AND SHE SHOOTS BETTER

Jennifer Smith grew up in the mountains of North Carolina, in a small town called Robbinsville. After her last two years of high school at a Georgia boarding school, she went to the University of South Carolina, where she nearly disappeared in the sea of students. It was there that she met a serviceman from Pelham, Alabama, a small town about fifteen miles south of Birmingham. At nineteen, after less than two unrewarding years of college, she married him and moved to Alabama.

Jennifer found herself a waitressing job in nearby Vestavia Hills, at a restaurant called Constantine's. Her marriage lasted only three years, and she would have run back home to the hills of Carolina, but her parents had moved and she felt that she had no home to go to. So she continued the waitressing, and her easy manner, blond hair, and good looks made her a popular fixture.

A lot of cops ate at Constantine's, and Jennifer always thought they seemed like nice guys. They were dedicated to their jobs, which seemed to give them some purpose. She admired that about them—it was something that was lacking in her own life. Slinging plates for a living was starting to lose its allure, and these guys certainly didn't seem any smarter than she was— but law enforcement was not exactly a wide-open field for women in the Deep South in the mid-seventies. In fact it was practically unheard of. Jennifer wasn't exactly frail physically, and she was a strong-willed young woman. She wanted something more in life, a job she could believe in. So she mentioned to the guys that she thought she would make a good police officer.

They looked at each other. Jennifer? The waitress? A cop? That's a good one. A big old state trooper leaned back and said with a laugh, "Honey, you couldn't even pass the entrance exam."

That was all she needed to hear. What was once an idle daydream quickly became a life goal. She arranged to take the entrance examination, and she passed with flying colors. The Jefferson County Sheriff's Department hired her in May 1976—making her only the third woman to be hired by the department. She was immediately assigned to the county jail, where she worked for two years as a matron. She knew she had to pay her dues.

In July 1978 Deputy Jennifer Smith was assigned to patrol. She thought it was fascinating work, and when the guys gave her a hard time, she gave it right back to them in spades. Once an escapee from an Illinois prison made his way down to the Birmingham area, kidnapped a girl from the parking lot of a shopping mall, raped her, and stole her car. Jennifer and her partner spotted the guy in the stolen car and gave chase. They hit speeds up to 110 miles per hour and then continued the chase. Jennifer got him after a breathless pursuit through a cornfield. She had certainly proved herself to her fellow officers.

Like so many cops, Jennifer got her first look at Jack Montgomery in the courthouse. She didn't know much about him, just that some fellow officers weren't exactly crazy about the guy. She thought that he was attractive, despite a twenty-year age difference between them. She asked around and found out he was married. So much for the rugged-looking older judge, she thought.

But after more time, she found herself hanging around in his courtroom, sometimes getting in on the judge's infamous after-court card games with bailiffs and lawyers. She learned a lot about the law, courtroom procedure, and Jack. "He was a terrible flirt, and he loved female attention," she said. He was still married to Sherry, but they weren't living together. He continued with his flirtations in open court, and in mid-1986 he asked her out.

It was nothing special, just dinner at his house before she had to go on patrol in nearby Cahaba Heights. He made soup and sandwiches and gave her a tour of his house. He was quite proud of all the changes he had made to the house, especially the bedroom, which he had enlarged. When she saw two large beds there, she was puzzled. He stammered that he couldn't stand to have anyone in his bed when he was trying to sleep. She later realized that was a crock—he was just embarrassed to admit that he had a separate bed for his dogs. That night he made a big deal about not kissing her good night because he was still married.

But she was absolutely smitten. She didn't think he was old— she thought he had a vitality and energy that most men half his age didn't possess.

And Jack, of course, was enthralled with the idea of dating a female cop, not to mention a younger, attractive, buxom cop. She hit all of the right buttons that Christmas when she gave him a Sig Sauer 9-millimeter handgun. She knew he was a gun nut, and he was thrilled with her gift. They would go to the county's firing range together, and she always shot better than he did. That made him proud of her and made her more of a catch.

They had an intense, whirlwind romance. Jack bought her presents and called her all of the time, saying he just needed to hear her voice. She also knew that he was intensely private. When his mother died that year, he went to Louisiana for the funeral but would not let Jennifer come. He didn't call for two weeks, but he sent her cards with syrupy inscriptions. At his insistence they didn't go out in public until his divorce from Sherry was final on Halloween 1986.

Jack and Jennifer were married January 3, 1987, in his house by Judge Sandra Ross Storm, a mutual friend. There were maybe ten friends in attendance, and the couple really didn't tell anyone else that they were getting married until after it was over. Jennifer's fellow officers were not shy about telling her that they thought it was a mistake. Many more of them did not like Jack. They thought he showed favoritism, especially in drug and gambling cases and especially when certain lawyers were involved. And judging from his courtroom demeanor, Jack did not exactly seem like perfect husband material. The other officers could only imagine what it was like to deal with his temper all of the time.

Their life at home, though, was surprisingly unremarkable, according to Jennifer. Jack was a homebody, and he had a thing for ordering merchandise from catalogs: clothes, cooking utensils, tools, and little electronic gadgets. He was a consumer. If it was new, he wanted it. He wasn't much for managing money and still had a sizable mortgage on the house.

Jack was usually very regimented. He woke up at seven o'clock every morning, started a pot of coffee, and turned on the TV for the morning news. He made one piece of toast with butter and jelly, cut it in half, and gave one half to the dogs. He laid his clothes out, took a shower, got dressed, and headed to work. He never spent more than half a day at work, but he never took any vacation either. He spent his afternoons running to the dry cleaners, the liquor store, or the drugstore. He'd buy a newspaper, come home, and read it in front of the TV.

For the first year, maybe two, Jack and Jennifer lived in a relatively happy house. Jack even gave up drinking for about six months. Jennifer marveled at how well he did his job, how quickly he could clear through a docket, and how easily he could absorb new case law and understand it immediately. Still she knew that he constantly upset people with his decisions and his courtroom behavior.

Then the drinking started back as bad as ever. Jack got moodier and was given a prescription for Xanax after he went to the hospital for heart problems and was diagnosed as suffering from post-traumatic stress syndrome. He even went to a psychologist to learn self-hypnosis and relaxation techniques, but nothing seemed to relieve his stress and depression. Meanwhile Jennifer, who had been promoted to lieutenant, was back on night shift and never seemed to get enough sleep. Jack now seemed very cold toward her—their whirlwind romance had petered out almost as quickly as it had appeared.

"I think Jack had terribly low self-esteem," Jennifer said. "He relied on theatrics and bullying in nearly every situation. The more I learned about victimology, the more I believed that he was abused as a child. One of the symptoms is a lack of feelings for others but a real selfishness about your own feelings. I'd tell him, 'You hurt that person's feelings,' but he never cared. Like it or lump it. But if somebody ticked him off, he'd become terribly rude, even out in public, to people he'd never met before."

Jennifer felt that she never really knew Jack, that he never truly let her inside. For someone so incapable of loving others, though, he certainly kept trying. In between his four wives in thirty-five years, he only spent five months unmarried. Like the lawyers and the defendants and the people who watched him on TV, Jack's wives were part of his audience. He needed their approval, and he needed to test them. If he could yell at them and mistreat them and they still came back, that showed him they loved him. If they didn't come back, he would simply find another.

"Jack loved female attention," Jennifer said, "but attention was all he needed." His dogs were the perfect companions for him. They gave affection to him unconditionally, and they asked for little in return. And there was so little that Jack could give.

CHAPTER FIFTEEN

NOT IN MY COURT

It was a rare occasion when Jack Montgomery stuck his foot so far in his mouth that he felt compelled to pull it out. That was the case in January 1989 after *Birmingham Post-Herald* reporter Joan Mazzolini reported that Jack and the other two district judges in the criminal division, O. L. "Pete" Johnson and Mike McCormick, had barred AIDS-infected defendants from appearing in their courtrooms. "I was surprised at how forthright Jack was about it," Mazzolini recalled. "I at least give him credit for being so honest about it. Maybe he didn't know at the time that it was a big deal. I was working on a story about something else, and he just came right out and told me. When I told someone at an AIDS clinic about it, they were appalled. I was appalled too."

The story of three hick judges in backward Alabama actually denying AIDS patients their days in court quickly went national. When the rest of the media moved in to develop the story further, Jack characteristically stepped up to the microphone and, as usual, made his feelings known.

In a radio interview Jack referred to gays as "flame queens" and said that "homosexuals were volunteering for AIDS." He said that those infected with the disease should be kept out of courtrooms because they might bite someone or become combative and spill their blood on others. (Of course Jack was a judge who had seen blood spilled in the courtroom before.)

Jack also said he thought the Centers for Disease Control and the medical establishment in general were keeping the truth about AIDS to themselves, masking infection numbers to prevent panic. "It's a cover-up. I just know it. I've got that gut feeling. I think they're dropping like flies."

Reaction was swift and vitriolic. A coalition of thirteen local and state organizations concerned with AIDS or the defendants' rights filed a complaint against the three judges, Jack in particular, with the state's Judicial Inquiry Commission (JIC). This was not the first time the JIC had received a complaint about Jack. In fact there had been at least three other complaints.

The JIC investigates hundreds of complaints against judges every year, most of them baseless. If the panel, made up of judges and lawyers appointed to the position, determined that an ethics violation had occurred, it filed charges that were then tried by another judges-only panel, the Court of the Judiciary. In more than twenty years, only twenty-seven cases had ever been sent to the Court of the Judiciary—usually the JIC found there was no basis or jurisdiction for the complaints. Sometimes, though, the investigation did get to the point where the panel requested the presence of the judge in question to get his version of events and probably issue a stern but private warning about the questionable behavior. Jack had been called before the JIC panel at least once before.

After the AIDS groups made it public that they had filed a complaint—which was their option despite the confidentiality of the judicial ethics system—Jack quickly realized that he had some placating to do. His wife Jennifer had already lit into him about the stupidity and hurtfulness of his comments, not to mention the fact that he was just plain wrong in asserting that AIDS infected gays only. She had also pointed out that his fears of transmission of the disease by combative defendants were remote at best. As usual Jack had not considered the feelings of others before opening his mouth. This was different, though—this time it put his job in jeopardy.

So Jack did something he had never done before—he publicly apologized. He sent a letter to the AIDS groups and then called a press conference to reemphasize the contents of the letter. "I will not discourage anyone from appearing in my courtroom, including AIDS patients," he wrote. "I have been taught now that homosexuals are not the only segment of our population at risk for AIDS, and I hope that members of the gay community will forgive this thoughtless comment."

Jack even promised that he would help the AIDS support groups in providing AIDS education within the judicial system and to the public. He later told a reporter, "My big problem is if I think it, it comes out of my mouth. Immediately. And that can get you into trouble."

Judges Johnson and McCormick did not give interviews throughout the controversy, but they did make it known that they had changed their courtroom policies soon after the publicity started.

"I'm surprised and pleased," Linda Potts, president of the AIDS Task Force of Alabama, said after the apology. "It's probably the best outcome we could have hoped for."

Jack did not, however, apologize specifically for the reference to "flame queens" because, quite simply, he never apologized for that kind of thing. "He really didn't have anything against gays," Jennifer said. "That was just the way he labeled people. It was backward and offensive to most people, but he never meant any ill will by it. He figured if you were gay, you should be proud to call yourself a flame queen. I think his apology was very genuine though. He realized he was wrong, and he realized he had to make things right."

The storm wasn't over, but the apology and change in courtroom policy had its effect: The AIDS groups informed the JIC that they were retracting their complaint against Jack. In fact, he did such a good job of apologizing that the groups only retracted their complaint against Jack, not the other two judges, because they had not publicly apologized for their anti-AIDS policies. The JIC, however, made it clear that there was no such thing as retracting a complaint. Once a complaint had been made and an investigation begun, the JIC saw it through to the end. And not all feathers in the AIDS support community had been smoothed.

After the apology Jack appeared at a meeting of AIDS caregivers. "They really jumped on him and took him to task," said Jennifer, who accompanied him to the meeting. "I think it was good for him. He remained calm and cordial through the whole thing, and he kept saying that they were right and he was wrong."

There was more humbling to be endured though. A little more than a week after he made the apology, Jack was relieved of his position as presiding district judge in the criminal division. The position was basically an administrative creation of the Jefferson County court system and carried very few responsibilities and no power, but it gave the appearance of losing a job. The decision was made at the annual meeting of the county's circuit judges, where they voted to take the job away from Jack and placed the duties with Joseph Jasper, presiding circuit judge. The circuit judges publicly said they did not feel that Jack should continue in that position since he was being investigated by the JIC. Privately, however, they knew that a JIC investigation was not that unusual. They simply saw this as an opportunity to slap Jack down for the AIDS incident as well as all his other inappropriate behavior.

When the JIC called Jack to appear before them, "he didn't sleep for days," Jennifer said. "He took those things very seriously. It worried him a lot because he knew they were the only ones who could actually take him off the bench." She went with him to meet with the JIC in Montgomery but could not go into the meeting with him. The panel questioned him for some time and then privately admonished him about his behavior, especially the public comments.

In April, Judges Johnson and McCormick made it known that they had received letters from the JIC saying the panel had found no basis for ethics charges. Jack at first would not say publicly if he had received such a letter. Then it was learned that his letter said his public comments about gays were "inappropriate, and they were apparently made on the basis of common misconceptions." Considering his policy change and his apology, though, the panel said, "your conduct does not warrant formal charges."

CHAPTER SIXTEEN

How Much?

Politically nobody challenged Jack Montgomery for his seat on the bench, but Birmingham mayor Richard Arrington made one attempt at challenging Jack's reputation and stature. Arrington was the city's first black mayor and had been in power for more than a decade. Issues, though, were not what they used to be, and despite a healthy machine and a firm grip on city hall, Arrington was getting clobbered publicly on crime. He was never much of a hands-on guy, especially when it came to the police department. By February 1991 the crime rate was operating at record levels, while the city's police chief was under indictment, charged with altering arrest records. The arrest in question was of Arrington's teenage daughter on a disorderly conduct charge. The mayor was never implicated in the charges of altering the records, but after a particularly nasty shoot-out in a housing project, he had to do something to demonstrate that he was addressing crime.

So Arrington called a rare press conference and did what executive officeholders have done since time immemorial—he blamed the courts. Specifically Arrington railed against what he said was an unwillingness of the local courts to set bonds high enough to keep dangerous criminals off the streets and in jail. No one at the press conference bothered to point out to the mayor that, except in rare cases, people charged but not yet convicted with committing crimes generally are entitled to bond and that the purpose of a bond is to ensure the defendant shows up for court. As an example of these "criminals being set free on bond to further terrorize law-abiding citizens," the mayor talked about a case brought to him by his detectives in the crimes against persons division, the case against Tony Scales.

Actually there was more than one case against Scales. At age thirty-one and already convicted years earlier of grand larceny, Scales was the focus of several police investigations into drug-related violence committed in the city's Kingston area, a haven for thugs and dealers. Forbidden by law from possessing a gun because of his previous conviction, Scales was arrested in November 1990 for having a stolen .38-caliber pistol, an AK47 assault rifle, a street sweeper shotgun, and two 9-millimeter machine pistols. He was released on $10,000 bond. A month later, while still out on bond, Scales was stopped by police in a rental car. They found another stolen pistol, another street sweeper, and an assault rifle in the trunk. That time he was denied bond. His lawyer, however, appealed the decision to a different judge, who set a $50,000 bond. Scales posted bond and was released.

In January the cops picked him up again. He was carrying three sticks of dynamite, blasting caps, and a pistol. Bond was again denied. This time Scales's attorney appealed the ruling to Jack, who had not dealt with the prior cases pending against Scales. He set bond at $100,000, and Scales was released. Shortly afterward Arrington called his press conference. He never mentioned Jack by name, but it did not take reporters long to figure out which judge turned Scales loose on the streets last, and they started calling Jack for comment about the mayor's attack on his actions.

Now the smart thing to do would have been to simply say that $100,000 was a lot for those charges and that it was twice the amount of bond last placed on Scales. Jack said those things, but he didn't stop there. First, he felt compelled to explain how it all happened, and in the process he made the whole thing sound so willy-nilly that it made people wonder if the system was working at all.

Jack said he had received a phone call at home from a lawyer asking him to establish a bond for Scales. "I recognized the voice, and I thought I knew who it was, but when I asked that person later, he said it wasn't him." So, Jack was saying that he had called the jail and ordered a bond for a defendant he had never met, under charges he had never seen on the say-so of an attorney he thought he was talking to. "We do lawyer and judge stuff by telephone all the time," Jack told the media. Somehow the system certainly didn't sound very effective at that point.

Then, probably out of insecurity and paranoia, Jack decided to go a step further with the media and get into a pissing match with Arrington. "He doesn't know what the fuck he's talking about," Jack said about the mayor. "I'd like to send everybody I get to Devil's Island and leave them there, but I can't do that. When Arrington gets a law degree, tell him he can come over and see me then. I'd be nowhere near being a good mayor. He should maybe not try to be a judge."

Arrington didn't miss the chance for a retort and said, "I understand how brilliant these people [judges] are, but I don't think I need a law degree to debate the issues. I can't have a judge sitting back there with a cigar stuck in his mouth telling the mayor to go to hell." Jack didn't smoke cigars, but the image was a strong one, and the media was eating this stuff up.

Jack went so far as to say the mayor's actions were irresponsible and actually causing damage to the process of setting bonds. "Arrington is doing more to hurt the criminal justice system than anybody, even the violent thugs. Before fucking with the criminal justice system, you've got to know it."

And then Arrington, Birmingham's first black mayor, put a racial spin on the issue and the loudmouthed white judge. "If

Tony were terrorizing Judge Montgomery or [District Attorney] David Barber's community instead of Kingston, would they treat him with kidskin gloves as they've done here? I think not. Bashing Arrington may be popular in some quarters, but people who don't understand that the violence of Kingston and Elyton Village [a housing project] is creeping closer to them are fools."

In his courtroom Jack heard a motion by the prosecution to reconsider the bond amount he set for Scales. He denied the motion, saying he still believed he did the right thing. Then the prosecutors took their motion over Jack's head to circuit court, where Judge Joseph Jasper revoked Scales's bond.

At the city council meeting the next week, Arrington opened fire again. The police department provided him with more information, and he aimed it right at Jack. He talked about two more accused criminals, Nathaniel Allen and Isaac Peterson. Allen had been charged with murder and attempted murder, and bond was set at $400,000, an amount that was too high for him to make. Allen's attorney unsuccessfully appealed the amount to the judge who set it. Two weeks later the attorney convinced Jack to lower the bond to $75,000, which Allen was able to make, and he was released.

Arrington did not know it at the time, but he and his detectives were really onto something. Two years later, when Jack was indicted on so many counts of bribery and extortion, the first two counts of the indictment claimed the judge agreed to lower bond for Tony Scales and Nathaniel Allen in exchange for money. Arrington didn't know that he had stepped into the middle of some little bribery scheme, but Jack certainly did. He must have been sweating bullets the whole time Arrington was hollering about him, thinking that the cops were getting close to his scheme. "I don't give a shit what he said about me," Jack said to a reporter. "It's really unimportant to me. I don't have any comment." That may well have been the only time Jack had actually said, "no comment," about anything.

The mayor also talked about the case of Isaac Peterson, who had been arrested a total of eight times over the previous eight months. All of the charges involved property crimes like burglary and receiving stolen property. He was a thief, a busy one, and each time he was hauled in, bond was set somewhere around $500, about average for a property crime. Each time he made bond and was turned loose. The last time he was charged was late January, and bond was set at $5,000, which he apparently could not make. A week later, though, Jack signed his bond, which was, in essence, a recognizance bond. Peterson got out of jail free.

Despite what had to be an absolute paranoia that he would be found out, Jack decided he was going to have the last word. No pip-squeak mayor was going to make him look like he was soft on crime. They thought his bonds were too low? He'd show them a bond they'd never forget. Isaac Peterson managed to get himself busted two days after he walked out of the jail on Jack's signature, and then he had the bad luck to land back in Jack's court on this new charge. With his usual flair for the dramatic, Jack set Peterson's bond at $9 trillion. The people at *The Guinness Book of Records* confirmed that it was, as best they could tell, the highest bond ever set. Suddenly Jack was the subject of national news reports again, not as a judge who set low bonds and let criminals walk and not as a judge who might be on the take, but as a judge who set the world's highest bond, and on a habitual thief.

"I didn't even think about Mayor Arrington," Jack said after setting the bond. "He's doing a great job. Leave him the fuck alone." Of course the number of people who believed that Jack set that bond without even thinking of the criticisms leveled at him just a week earlier could have played Twister in a phone booth. But that was his story, and by God, he stuck to it. He said he set such a high bond because Peterson "broke one of my cardinal rules. If I recognize you on a bond and you go out and pick up another case, then you got me to deal with again. It's generally no bond, but this time I just picked $9 trillion for no particular reason other than it came to my mind."

The next day Peterson's attorney, former prosecutor George Andrews, appeared in Jack's court and asked the judge to reduce his client's outlandish bond. Jack smiled and told Andrews that he would be happy to cut the bond amount in half. Andrews said he thought that would still be "somewhat excessive." Even Bill Neuman, the soft-spoken deputy district attorney assigned to Jack's court, couldn't bring himself to say he was happy with the $9 trillion, but he was not about to cross Jack on something he was obviously having so much fun with. Neuman declined to recommend a specific amount from the prosecution but did say he did not think Peterson should be let out of jail.

"You've got six pendings and two priors," Jack told Peterson. "The bond remains the same." Of course the bond was greatly reduced on appeal, but Jack knew that didn't matter. He went down on record as the judge who set the world's largest bond. Nobody even remembered what Arrington had been complaining about. Jack felt so good that he even took the opportunity to play aw-shucks about it all. "I'm just a local country jerk. I don't have any business getting on the national media for doing something like that."

Locally the media put out another round of features about Jack describing him as flamboyant and brash. In one of those stories, Jack said he didn't mind professional criticism, "but when you attack me personally, I'm going to come get you, whip your ass, and do anything I can to shove your spine in your ear." Of course, Jack took everything personally.

CHAPTER SEVENTEEN

PUPPY LOVE

At the same time Jack Montgomery's fourth marriage started coming apart, he took an interest in a young lawyer who began trolling for cases in his courtroom. Wendy Williams was fresh out of Birmingham School of Law. She had been working for attorney Chris Christ, one of her instructors in law school. He was nagging Wendy to bring in new business, but she just didn't seem to have the knack for that yet. So she packed up her books and went into practice for herself, working out of her apartment. Now she had to drum up clients, and she decided to take appointed cases. Wendy had heard about Jack and his moods from her former boss. She had heard that the judge didn't like new lawyers, and he didn't like women lawyers. She had heard that he did what he could to embarrass lawyers he didn't like, but she was desperate for work.

"When I was introduced to Jack, he had a Coke in his hand," Wendy remembered. "He smiled at me, put his arm around me, and said, 'We'll take good care of you.' I was thinking, that certainly wasn't as bad as I thought it was going to be."

Wendy got a few cases assigned to her and met Attorney Scott Boudreaux, a friend of Jack's. Boudreaux was looking for an attorney to share his office space, and by March 1990, Williams was moved in and had a small client base going.

Jack had remained cordial but businesslike with Wendy so far. One time in his court, she was appointed to a case in which the defendant had been videotaped by the police making a drug deal. Wendy motioned for a continuance of the preliminary hearing so she could view the tape. Jack responded, "Hell, no, I'm not continuing this."

"Fine," she said, "then I waive the preliminary hearing."

Wendy quickly realized that Jack's bluster was his way of teaching young lawyers who were paying attention. He wanted people in his courtroom who moved fast and knew what they were doing. She studied hard and quickly fell into the pace. In an effort to get to know more people around the courthouse and make more connections, she started hanging around after Jack concluded court for the day to get in on the bull sessions with the judge and other lawyers.

One day Jack asked Wendy, "How would you like to be on TV?" He said the morning show on WBRC–TV Channel 6, now with new hosts, had been calling him and asking him if he'd return to the show. He said he couldn't but he'd try to find someone else. Even though she was far from experienced in the courtroom and had no experience working in television, she knew an opportunity when she heard one. Jack took her up Red Mountain to the TV station in the big white house, where he introduced her around as "the female Jack Montgomery." Wendy was a regular guest on the show for about a year.

Meanwhile Jack continued to tutor Wendy about the law. At home, he often talked about what he called the "baby lawyers" and the progress they were making. His wife Jennifer said she heard him talk about Wendy Williams several times and how the young lawyer could "talk about explicit sexual things" with the best of them.

"I could talk to him without worrying about the conse-quences," Wendy said. "We were very open with each other." Jack finally asked her to lunch, and she didn't respond. He said, "You don't have a hair on you if you don't." Wendy couldn't resist that kind of dare and agreed.

They walked out to his white Cherokee, and he opened the door for her. "He drove like a bat out of hell," Wendy recalled with a laugh. Jack took her to Michael's, an old, established steakhouse on Birmingham's Southside, the kind of place where people went because their parents used to go there and the waiters knew the names of all of the regulars. Jack talked about his wife Jennifer most of the time. He said they both were fanatics about guns. At one point, he said Jennifer had encouraged his friendship with Wendy.

On the way back to the courthouse, Jack asked, "Would you consider dating me if I wasn't married?" Wendy thought about it for a second and said, "Probably." Jack was almost sixty years old. Wendy was twenty-nine.

Wendy had golden blond hair and sparkling blue eyes. She was overweight but hid the extra pounds well under her business suits. She had a small mouth with full lips that were drawn up like a bow, and she had a hearty laugh. Jack was smitten with her.

Wendy had not had the easiest of upbringings. Her father was an insurance agent who was always gone. When he was home, he drank. The family moved every couple of years. Then her parents divorced when she was eleven. She moved with her mother and her autistic younger sister from Columbus, Georgia, back to her mother's hometown near Birmingham. Within a couple of years, her mother married her high school sweetheart, who had two daughters and a son. They moved to a small apartment in Fairfield, Alabama, a struggling city in the west end of Jefferson County that was built on the back of the steel industry. In less than a year, they moved into a house in Ensley, a community in western Birmingham that was also dying as the vines grew over the dormant steel plants. Wendy had a little more room to breathe at home and went to Ensley High School with the grandchildren of the Italian immigrants who had worked in the plants.

Jennifer noticed that Jack was coming home late more and more often, and she knew it was because of Wendy Williams. She said that Jack insisted he did not want a divorce, "but he forced me into it." The sheriff's office sent her on a trip to Huntsville for several days at the end of July 1990, not long after Jack and Wendy's lunch together. "He asked me if it was OK to take her to dinner, and I told him no, it was not OK," Jennifer said. "I was unable to reach him on the phone two or three nights while I was gone."

When Jennifer got back home, Jack sauntered in from the pool without saying a word. They argued through August. That month, Wendy said, Jennifer called her one night and asked her to come over to the house. Jack met Wendy outside right after she drove up. They talked for a moment and then walked inside to face Jennifer. The three of them sat at the dining room table, and Jennifer made it clear that she wanted some answers. "I remember thinking, 'Why am I here?'" Wendy said. "The first thing she asked was where did I think this relationship was going. I said, 'We're friends. That's all.'"

The conversation lasted until four o'clock in the morning, Wendy said, and Jack never did say much.

Jennifer, however, remembered that Jack and Wendy whispered and giggled with each other the whole night. They didn't notice Jennifer unless Jennifer addressed them. Jennifer got more and more pissed off the longer she watched this display. "I had a couple of choices that night, and I chose to drink a lot," she said. That seemed like the least violent choice available—otherwise, she felt she might make a really ugly scene.

Just days later Jack rented an apartment, supposedly for him to use during a trial separation. On September 1, though, Jennifer moved into the apartment. "He was having a late-life crisis," she said. "The thought of turning sixty was driving him crazy. He felt like life had passed him by."

Around that time Jack decided to dye his gray body hair, Jennifer said. On October 12 she filed for divorce. Her complaint claimed an "incompatibility of temperament" and an "irretrievable breakdown of this marriage. We argue over financial matters and each other's behavior as to work and do not agree as to any social activities mutually. Because of these arguments, we are unable to live together in any form of harmony, and the disagreements are affecting our physical and mental well-being." Nowhere did the complaint mention Wendy Williams by name or another woman in general, but Jennifer said that was the heart of the problem.

After the divorce Jack and Wendy openly became a couple. They went to the judges' Christmas dinner that year. Sandra Ross Storm, the judge who had performed Jack and Jennifer's wedding ceremony, remembered seeing Jack and Wendy at the dinner. That did not give her as much pause as Jack's behavior that night. "He came around to our table and talked about how much he loved being a judge and how much he loved the rest of us. He said he felt like we were a family. I'd never heard him talk like that before. He even cried a little. For the longest time, I thought that was the most bizarre thing I'd ever seen Jack do. I don't even think he was drinking that night. I know he wasn't drunk. But it was just so weird. It was like he was saying good-bye to us or something."

What Storm didn't know was that Wendy had touched a nerve in Jack. The affection of this young woman came at such an unstable point in his life that it had actually caused Jack to get in touch with some of his emotions. He may not have known what to do with those emotions, but more than one person noticed a change in Jack.

As for the fact that Jack and Wendy were together in public, "I don't know what people thought," Wendy said. "The more I was with him, the more I didn't care what people thought.

He was never an old-thinking person. I never really thought about the age difference. For a judge, I thought he was really very nonjudgmental."

Not long after New Year's, Jack paid a visit to Wendy's mother and asked for her permission to propose to Wendy, and she gave it. "On February 23 he came to my place, and he got down on one knee," Wendy said. "He was almost in tears when he asked me. I think I knew he was going to ask me sooner or later, but when he did, all I could think was, 'Oh, shit.' I was stunned I think, and I was back to worrying about what others would think. I loved him as a person. Was I in love with him? Probably." Wendy had never really had a serious relationship with a man before so she did not have much experience to rely on. She agreed to marry him.

They were married July 12, 1991, at the posh, old Southern-style Donnelly House in Birmingham's garden district on Highland Avenue. Wendy had slimmed down and looked stunning in her classic wedding dress. They did it traditionally and invited quite a few people, including, of course, lawyers and judges and even excons. "I knew I was going to do it only once," Wendy said. "So I wanted to do it right and do it big."

As their marriage began, Wendy felt the eyes and the innuendos at the courthouse. She knew some people thought she was a judicial gold digger, marrying the old man to get a leg up in court. So she went out of her way to dispel those perceptions. Jack wanted her to park in the judges' parking lot. She didn't want the special treatment. She kept her last name too, partly because Jennifer had not dropped the "Montgomery" from her name, partly because she didn't want to rub the connection in people's faces.

About a year later, however, the connection came up publicly after Jack had Wendy put on his short list of substitute judges. Steve Visser of *The Birmingham News* wrote a story about the judge's wife, just four years out of law school, sitting on the bench in district court. "That was his way of starting me on the road to becoming a judge," Wendy recalled. "I didn't really understand what the problem was then, but I guess a lot of people were jealous." For Jack, he had given Wendy what was certainly his most prized possession, his seat on the bench.

"I'll admit, their relationship was close," Jennifer said. "I think she reached him like nobody had before, maybe because they were so much alike. He was crazy about her, and she could get him to do new things, go out to new places. I could never get him to do any of that. I think they understood each other from the start." Jack went to restaurants on the trendy Southside with Wendy, and he socialized with her younger friends. Also, Jack opened up to Wendy about his father and told her about the pain he felt his whole life because of Jack Sr.

CHAPTER EIGHTEEN

FOR DOUG

Usually local police officers and federal agents aren't the best of friends. The cops think the feds are too full of self-importance because they show up in the middle of an investigation and tend to take over. Mark Hobbs didn't have that reaction to Doug Althouse though. Hobbs was an undercover narcotics sergeant with the police department in Hoover, a bustling, upscale suburb south of Birmingham. He was setting up a $50,000 buy when Althouse, a fairly new agent with the federal Drug Enforcement Agency (DEA), was brought in on the case. They all sat down, Hobbs laid out the plan, and Althouse said simply, "Sounds good. Let's do it."

"We hit it off from there," Hobbs recalled. "We just gelled perfectly." As the cop and the fed worked other cases together, they became friends and their personal lives became intertwined. When Althouse was having trouble in his marriage, Hobbs loaned him his house while he and his own wife vacationed in the mountains.

They started working a case on a reputed multikilo cocaine dealer named Richard Morrow. Through their investigation, Hobbs and Althouse knew Morrow had a comfortable but not flashy house north of Birmingham and an apartment on the city's Southside. But they also knew they didn't have the full story—Morrow had to have a stash house. Where was it? They tailed him for days at a time, hoping he would unknowingly lead them to the stash house, but he never did.

The investigators developed a professional respect for Morrow—he was good at what he did. He just stayed in the game a little too long, and they knew they were going to get him sooner or later. For the most part, though, Morrow played it just right—he kept the business in the family so no one would turn him in, he kept the operation low-key and diversified, and he kept his head low.

Finally Hobbs and Althouse just said the heck with the stash house. They had enough evidence to take Morrow and his family down, and that's what they planned to do. Still, having that house would not only yield a goodly amount of drugs, it would also have completed the evidentiary picture of a drug operation that dealt in millions of dollars a year.

On May 28, 1992, Althouse was tied up with another case during the day, but Hobbs continued to tail Morrow. Hobbs called Althouse a few times to tell him he was having a productive day but still hadn't found Morrow's stash house. That evening Hobbs met with the tactical squad that was going to help the investigators serve search warrants on both of Morrow's locations simultaneously. It was going to be a tricky operation, and it took a lot of detailed planning. Hobbs and Althouse were going to meet later that night and discuss the meeting with the tactical squad and tie up any loose ends before serving the search warrants in the next couple of days.

During the meeting with the tactical squad, one of the officers received a phone call from his wife. She told him that a DEA agent had been shot in the parking lot of the Chevron Food Mart on U.S. 280 in northern Shelby County, a residential area just east of Hoover. "I knew right away that it was Althouse," Hobbs said.

He jumped into his car and raced toward the convenience store. Over his police radio Hobbs heard that the agent died at the scene. He became so frantic, yelling over the radio, that the voices on the other end did their best to talk him off the road. Hobbs did pull over and compose himself for a few minutes before speeding down U.S. 280 to the crime scene. The only thing he could think was that Morrow had found out about the investigation and had arranged to have Althouse hit.

When Hobbs arrived at the convenience store, a light rain was falling on Althouse's body, which was lying on the black pavement, draped with a sheet of plastic. At age twenty-eight, the gung ho DEA officer had been killed by a single shot to the chest, not during an act of retribution by Morrow or another drug dealer running scared but by a kid who only wanted the black Camaro Z28 Althouse was sitting in. Eugene Clemons, twenty-one, had no idea he had shot a federal agent until he heard the news the next day.

Even now, years later, talking about Althouse's death still causes Hobbs to shake uncontrollably, as if he were locked out in a snowstorm in a T-shirt. Sometimes tears stream down his cheeks.

The investigation into Althouse's murder was the jurisdiction of the FBI, and they wrapped it up fairly quickly. Hobbs went to Althouse's hometown in Pennsylvania for the funeral. After he boarded the plane to return to Birmingham, Hobbs decided that his first order of business was going to be Morrow. It was the last case he had worked on with Althouse, and he was determined to complete it. Morrow was going to do his time—for Doug Althouse.

Back in Birmingham, Hobbs had to pick up Morrow's scent again, just to test the waters and make sure that he and the tactical team wouldn't storm into something they weren't ready for. He had tailed Morrow for a day when suddenly he found himself being led to an unfamiliar location, a condo in Homewood—it was Morrow's stash house.

"He drove me straight to it," Hobbs said. "I couldn't believe it. It was just so sweet. I wanted more than anything to tell Doug Althouse."

The police and federal agents hit all three locations at the same time. They arrested Morrow and found cocaine and marijuana everywhere, even in the box springs of a bed in the condo. Six empty kilo wrappers made from a Spanish-language newspaper told them that their haul could have been even bigger. But Hobbs had Morrow cold, and that's all he wanted.

Oddly they did not find much cash. And when Hobbs asked Morrow where all his money was, Morrow laughed and said he didn't have any money, despite the fact that he bought new cars with cash on almost a monthly basis. This guy, Hobbs thought, was going to be set for life when he got out of prison. Of course he was certain that a drug dealer this big would be in prison for quite a while.

The case against Richard Morrow landed in Jack's court-room to be passed on to a grand jury. "I had been in Jack Montgomery's courtroom before," Hobbs said. "I had witnessed all of his antics, but I thought they were just that. As far as I knew, law enforcement considered him a friend.

"When I was a rookie, I saw a lawyer arguing his client's bond before Jack, and Jack had leaned forward and said to the lawyer, 'You know what? You're just trying to fuck with the system. Well, I'll show you how the system can fuck with you. Your client has no bond.' I thought that was pretty funny. I knew if you didn't do your job or you got on his bad side, he'd hammer you. But I did my job. Walking in, I wasn't worried."

But instead of a hearing to send Morrow to the grand jury, Hobbs walked into a private meeting with Jack and Morrow. The judge told Hobbs, "Son, I'm going to do you a big favor. I'm going to make you a big hero," and a shiver went down Hobbs's spine. Jack told Hobbs that he wasn't going to send Morrow's case any further in order to let Morrow snitch for Hobbs. Arresting twenty drug dealers was a lot better than arresting just one, wasn't it? Hobbs was skeptical, but what could he say to a judge?

Jack said he had raised Morrow's $250,000 bond to $500,000 to scare him a bit, to set him up for the informant deal. Jack put Hobbs in his chambers alone with Morrow to work it out. When they finished, Jack asked if everyone was happy, and they said they were. Jack then lowered Morrow's bond to $25,000, which Morrow made. That, Jack told Hobbs, was to show Morrow that good things would happen to him if he cooperated.

Hobbs didn't think Morrow could do him any good, and it didn't take Morrow long to prove Hobbs's suspicions correct. Even before Jack's deal with Morrow, this case was starting to smell funky to Hobbs. Attorney John Robbins, who had been retained by Morrow, called Hobbs before the scheduled hearing and asked him what was going on—why Morrow had fired him and hired Attorney Greg Jones. He said Jones had practically stolen Morrow from under his nose at the county jail, and Jones was with bail bondsman Warren King. Morrow's wife paid Robbins a retainer one minute and then asked for it back the next. When Robbins showed up in Jack's office to let the court know he was Morrow's attorney, the judge was abusive to him and said he had heard Morrow's name coming up too much lately. At the initial hearing later in the day, Jack said to Morrow, "You've got more lawyers than Noriega. I've had all kinds of lawyers come into my office talking about you. Who's your lawyer?" Morrow said it was Greg Jones. Hobbs said he had no idea what was going on, but he wondered.

Even though Morrow had signed an agreement to be an informant for Hobbs, he kept missing appointments and failed to come up with anything usable. At the same time, Jack kept paging Hobbs to ask how Morrow was doing. Hobbs had never seen a judge show this kind of interest in a case before, and he simply didn't know what to make of it. Finally he called Morrow and told him that he had stiffed him for the last time. "Morrow, it's just not going to happen. I'm not going to try to work with you. I'm through with you," he said and hung up. Within minutes Jack paged Hobbs.

Hobbs told Jack that the informant deal wasn't working—Morrow had not put forth any effort, and he was thinking about turning the case over to the DEA to have Morrow prosecuted in federal court. Jack said, "Wait—me and Warren King went out last night and talked to Richard. He's going to straighten up." Hobbs knew right then what he had, and he felt sick.

Jack gave Hobbs King's phone number and told him to arrange a meeting with all of them in Jack's chambers to show Morrow that they meant business about this informant thing. "Oh, and by the way," he said, "what are you going to do with that Mercedes you took from Morrow?" Hobbs said he was eventually going to put it up for auction like all confiscated drug dealer cars. Jack then suggested that Hobbs let Morrow have it back in order to keep up appearances and his value as an informant.

Hobbs couldn't believe he was hearing this. He told Jack that he was not, under any circumstances, going to let Morrow have his car back. Hobbs then called King to set up the meeting, and King told Hobbs that he needed to let Morrow start selling drugs again before he could be any good as an informant. Hobbs thought that even a slow-witted bail bondsman knew that would be illegal.

"All I could think was that I had big problems," Hobbs recalled. "Politically I was way out of my league, and I had to figure out what to do." That night he and his partner, Ray Chaffin, stayed up in Hobbs's kitchen, drinking coffee and discussing their options. "We were in a heckuva jam. This judge was dirty, and he had corrupted the case. The look in Ray's eyes told me that he didn't want to be here at all. If we ignored all of this and Jack Montgomery got caught, we could go to prison too. And if we tried to turn him in, that could be it for us."

Even the most cynical person would have trouble believing that Hobbs could be part of anything underhanded. In his early thirties at the time, Hobbs had a chiseled, All-American face. He looked like the kind of guy who, if he showed up on the front porch for a date, the girl's dad would slip ten bucks into his hand for a pizza after the movie. He had been the captain of his football team at Ensley High School in western Birmingham. The fact that Hobbs could conduct undercover drug cases with a face that would be perfect for milk commercials may have been his greatest feat.

But now, faced with an obvious question of right and wrong, those two choices did not look so clear. Hobbs thought about his daughter Jessica, who was six at the time. Would he be putting her in danger? He thought about Althouse and their case that was being flushed before his eyes. "The very last thing I wanted to do at that point in my life was take on a judge," he said.

After looking at it every way they could, Hobbs and Chaffin decided to call Bob McGregor, who worked in the U.S. Attorney's office. Hobbs knew Battlin' Bob from McGregor's days in the Jefferson County District Attorney's office. What Hobbs didn't know was that McGregor had been waiting several years for this very phone call.

McGregor is one of those people who claim they not only knew Jack was nuts but also that he was dirty. McGregor had a neverending supply of indignation and bile. Many people who are faced with injustice or insanity on a daily basis eventually give in to it and for their own sanity, let it wash over them. But even after ten years as a prosecutor, McGregor could still get red in the face and look at you incredulously as if he's never before heard anything so outlandish, when in fact he'd heard stuff twice that bad.

"When I got my first look at Jack, I thought, this is one crazy son of a bitch," McGregor recalled. "He impressed me as a blowhard and a bully. He used and abused people, and that made me angry."

In 1986 Lee Bragan was a deputy district attorney directly under McGregor's supervision. He was a hard-charging young prosecutor, and, as McGregor put it, a crook. Bragan was caught trying to extort money from Defense Attorney Mark Polson, who was representing a woman charged with cocaine possession. Bragan had told Polson that he would be happy to recommend a fairly lenient split sentence for the woman in exchange for $500.

During the investigation into Bragan's attempted extortion, word got around the courthouse that in addition to Bragan a judge was being scrutinized. One night McGregor and a colleague went down the list of jurists trying to figure out who the FBI might have on the line. "We got to Jack Montgomery's name, and we both stopped and looked at each other. I said, 'I'm telling you, he's in the perfect position, and he has no morals. He's on the take. It all makes sense now.'"

Later McGregor had himself or heard about other run-ins with Jack, not just personality conflicts but actual miscarriages of justice. There was always an odor about those cases, like the Nickey Charles Freeman murder case.

Then there was Teresa Pulliam. She had been a deputy district attorney in Mobile County when McGregor worked there, and they had both suffered through the reign of a judge on the take. When McGregor went north to Jefferson County, Teresa did too. They were good friends, and she possessed the same kind of passionate distaste for injustice that McGregor did. She had endured her share of run-ins with Jack, at least partly because she was a woman.

Once she had a rape case in which the victim was the girl-friend of a notorious drug dealer. A total of eight defendants, including the drug dealer, were charged with the rape and sodomy of the woman. They had burned her with heated coat-hangers, and the drug dealer had urinated on her. She had finally escaped by jumping out of a second-story window, stark naked. The preliminary hearing was held in Jack's courtroom. The place was packed with the drug dealer's cohorts, and the atmosphere was raucous—the victim was frightened out of her mind. Pulliam put the victim on the stand, but Jack did not wait long to move in. He started questioning the girl himself, harshly, crudely, at a rapid pace. It rattled her to the point that she couldn't keep the events straight in her head. Pulliam told a few officers in the courtroom to take notes since there was no reporter, which meant there was no record of the proceedings. When Pulliam asked for a break, Jack stood up, looked at the girl sobbing on the stand, and said, "You're the worst goddamn fucking witness I have ever seen."

Another time Pulliam stood quietly while Jack ranted and raved at her and threatened to throw her in jail. "He was so red, I thought he might shoot me," she said. "I almost wanted him to do something to me. He was a disgrace, and everybody who went into that courtroom regularly knew it."

When it became known that McGregor was moving to the U.S. Attorney's office, Pulliam stopped by his office on one of his last days in the county courthouse. She leaned into his office and said, "Bob, make me one promise before you go. Promise me that if the chance comes, you'll get that bastard

Jack Montgomery." McGregor promised, never thinking that the chance would fall into his lap. But here were two young officers, absolutely wide-eyed with fright. They knew they had Jack, they just didn't know what to do with him.

McGregor knew. He called Steve Brannan, an FBI agent McGregor had worked with before and trusted. He handed the phone to Hobbs, and Brannan asked Hobbs if he would wear a wire to the meeting with Jack. Hobbs said he would.

CHAPTER NINETEEN

THE QUIET AGENT

When Steve Brannan skippered a small navy riverboat in the Mekong Delta of Vietnam, he once overheard one of his crewmen tell another, "That Lieutenant Brannan—I bet he wouldn't say 'shit' if his mouth was full of it."

Brannan was not exactly a rough-and-tumble guy. He was raised in the small town of Tallassee, Alabama—three square blocks on Main Street with a barber shop and a post office. When young Brannan needed to cross the street, he'd simply wait at the corner until a police officer walked out and escorted him. Brannan's father pastored at the town's Church of Christ, and the family lived in the parsonage next door. Steve was raised to be a strict Christian and a pacifist. When he was ten, the family moved to Montgomery so his father could start a church to serve the students at Alabama Christian College.

Early on Brannan wanted to be a doctor, but his college grades weren't good enough to get him into medical school. So his butt belonged to Uncle Sam. He decided to enlist rather than wait for the draft. He wanted to fly, but the navy determined that his eyesight wasn't good enough. He went to Officers Candidate School and then volunteered to pilot a riverboat. People thought he was crazy to do it, but his cousin was killed in Vietnam, and Brannan wanted to see what it was all about. When he got out on the choppy waters of the South China Sea, Brannan found out something very important about himself: He was a flasher. Flashing is the navy term for seasickness, and Brannan was going for the unit flash record. When the opportunity arrived, he volunteered to take his patrol boat up the calm river waters of the delta. Yes, that's where all the shooting was, but something had to be better than puking his guts out all the time.

"We'd get into the shooting pretty regularly," Brannan recalled, "but none of our crew was ever killed or hurt badly. We went all over. We were on the Cambodian border for four months. We searched everything that came and went. At night, we deposited SEALS and set up ambushes."

Brannan came back to the world in 1969 wearing a commendation medal with a leaf for valor. He was then assigned to be a navy recruiter on college campuses in Alabama and Mississippi. Times being what they were, that was not exactly an easy assignment. He was thrown off the Jackson State campus. At the all-black Tuskegee College someone put a sign up behind him that said, "I want you, nigger." At Ole Miss, he was approached by a couple of football players. One of them told him that the hippies had given a Marine recruiter a hard time a couple of weeks ago, and then he gave Brannan his phone number and told him to call if he needed any help. Brannan's little recruiting table was on the balcony of the school's rotunda. Sure enough, a group of kids came by after a while and started hassling Brannan and throwing ketchup on his recruiting materials. Just then the football players came up behind the group and pitched two of them over the balcony. The rest ran. "Why didn't you call me?" the beefy kid asked Brannan. "I ... I don't have a phone here," Brannan stammered.

Two years of that, and Brannan decided it was time to look for a new occupation. He had an uncle who was a cop in Montgomery, and his uncle always said he loved law enforcement. A good friend of his was an FBI agent. "By then, I knew I could get shot at and still do my job," Brannan recalled. "I was never really worried about the bullet with my name on it—the one that worried me was the one addressed, 'To whom it may concern.' "

Brannan took the FBI exam in 1971 and stayed in the navy on a month-to-month basis. By mid-1972, he was in Quantico, Virginia, as a probationary agent. FBI Director J. Edgar Hoover died during Brannan's first week at the academy, and Brannan was engaged at the time. Because his was the first class to go through the new facility, it seemed like they spent half the time policing the area and putting together bunk beds. When he finished the sixteen-week training course, he was issued his official FBI badge and briefcase. On the sheet that asked where he would like to be stationed, Brannan put down Miami. So the FBI sent him to Minneapolis.

The Vietnam veteran was assigned to work selective service cases—draft dodgers. His first case was an old dog, a guy who skipped to Canada in 1968. Brannan thought he'd show everybody, he'd catch this guy when nobody else had. He decided to go talk to the suspect's mother, but his training agent didn't have time to go with him. "Look, talk to the neighbors first. And when you go to his house, ask for him before you identify yourself," the older agent advised.

Brannan drove out to the mother's neighborhood and trudged through the eighteen inches of snow on the ground talking to neighbors. One of them said he was pretty sure that the guy Brannan was looking for was in his mother's house. Brannan knocked on the mother's door, and the draft dodger answered, wearing only his pajama bottoms. Brannan gave some kind of greeting, and they shook hands. That's when Brannan clicked the handcuffs around the guy's wrist. "You sure like arresting people, don't you?" the dodger asked as they walked out to Brannan's car. "Look at that smile on your face." Once back at the office, all the training officer could do was give Brannan a hard time about making the arrest himself.

Brannan got married in Walker County, Alabama, and brought his wife to Minneapolis. She hated the cold weather and absolutely refused to drive in the snow. In 1973 he was assigned to the siege at Wounded Knee, where he worked roadblock duty twenty-four hours on, twelve hours off. Every once in a while, snipers from the Sioux nation took potshots at him. Otherwise the duty consisted largely of boredom. He got a furnished apartment on a month-to-month lease and had his wife come out to South Dakota to stay with him. One of his superiors told him that he would have to send his wife back because it was bad for the morale of the other men. Brannan, who usually tried to follow the rules, refused and challenged the supervisor to bring him up on charges. Instead, they spent the rest of Wounded Knee trying to make each other miserable. Usually the supervisor won, giving Brannan the worst assignments, like two straight weeks doing surveillance from a church steeple.

Brannan was transferred to the Sioux Falls office, and while he was there, he was assigned to a fugitive case. The guy had killed two people during a bar robbery, stolen an airplane from the Birmingham, Alabama, airport, and later shot a trooper. The fugitive had not been known to have been in the Sioux Falls area since that time, but Brannan wanted to find him. He went to the apartment complex where the guy used to live and asked the manager for the names and apartment numbers of the tenants who were living there five years earlier. He started knocking on doors at night, showing the fugitive's picture around.

One woman didn't recognize the name of the fugitive, but when Brannan showed her the picture, she said, "Oh, my God, that's my fiancé." She had a phone number for him in Fort Lauderdale. Brannan did some digging and found out the guy had been married six times without ever getting a divorce. One day the woman called Brannan at his office and said her fiancé was back in Sioux Falls and staying at a local hotel.

Brannan got out there with the SWAT team. They fired tear gas into the hotel room, and then they heard a pop—the guy had killed himself on the bed. Brannan's office got a $4,000 bill from the hotel.

When Brannan was transferred to the Detroit FBI office, his wife cried for two days because she wanted so badly to get out of the Snowbelt. Brannan was assigned to the security squad, European sector. He was supposed to identify communist spies, and he couldn't even talk with his wife about his work. Within three months, a big break simply fell into his lap, something he can't talk about even now. But it was so big that suddenly he was the expert on communist spies, teaching classes at Quantico. He then worked security out of Ann Arbor, Michigan, until 1984, when an opening came up in the Birmingham, Alabama, office. Finally he could take his wife home. He worked security in Birmingham for two years but was itching to do work that was a little more in the public eye. The preacher's son who never took anything stronger than NyQuil was then assigned to the narcotics division.

He had been there six months with no major action when a public corruption case landed in the Birmingham office. A lobbyist by the name of Hugh Boles was passing out shares of Birmingham's new horse track to public officials, especially legislators. With his long background in security, Brannan was assigned to the case. After months of work, Brannan developed enough for charges against several legislators. Boles pled guilty; the rest were acquitted.

Brannan's superiors were not disappointed by his work however. He had tenacity and the ability to deal with the extreme bureaucracy involved in public corruption cases. Perhaps Brannan's most effective weapons were his appearance and his demeanor. He was sleight of build, had gray hair combed to the side, and wore glasses. He looked like Steve Martin's nerdy older brother, and he had a way of speaking, a gentleness to his voice that was soothing to hear. He was so quiet that you would be tempted to take bets that he couldn't yell if his life depended upon it. This guy didn't just seem like the preacher's son—he seemed like the preacher. You could almost see him in the kindergarten class at church reading the kids a Bible story for naptime, the kids yawning as his voice lulled them into slumber.

Brannan successfully investigated the case of Alabama State Representative Pat Davis, who was convicted of attempting to extort $25,000 from the United Mine Workers in exchange for moving the Buy Alabama Coal bill out of her committee. Then he was made the lead Birmingham investigator in the December 1989 bombing death of U.S. Circuit Judge Robert Vance, the same Robert Vance who had delivered the message to put Jack on the bench years earlier. A pipe bomb had arrived in the mail, and Vance had opened it in the kitchen of his home in Mountain Brook, the old-money community that lies on the southeast border of Birmingham. Within two days another bomb arrived, but did not explode, at the courthouse of the Eleventh U.S. Circuit Court of Appeals in Atlanta, where Vance sat. A third bomb arrived at the Savannah law office of Robbie Robinson, who died shortly after opening the package. A Georgia malcontent named Walter Leroy Moody was finally arrested after one of the most extensive federal investigations in U.S. history.

McGregor made the right decision when he called Brannan to help Mark Hobbs and Ray Chaffin catch Jack in taking bribes. If anybody knew how to catch a crooked judge, Brannan did. "Steve was a damn good agent," McGregor said. "I was impressed with his work on other cases, and this one was going to take finesse and patience. I'll admit it, I had a personal interest in this case. Yeah, I wanted the son of a bitch off the bench."

CHAPTER TWENTY

A GIFT FROM HEAVEN

After talking to Steve Brannan on Bob McGregor's phone that night, Mark Hobbs agreed to take a concealed tape recorder to the meeting with Jack Montgonery, King, and Morrow the next day. "At the meeting, I said to [Jack] Montgomery, 'Judge, this case is very important to me,' and I told him why, about me and Doug. He told me about Korea, where he'd lost a lot of good buddies and that he understood but life goes on. I laid out every clue I could, telling him, Judge, don't mess with this case."

Jack laid out a clue of his own, more like bait, to see if Hobbs would bite. He started talking about Birmingham's most notorious drug dealer, Otha Taylor, who was convicted a few years earlier. He said he performed the marriage of Otha and his girlfriend while Otha was in the county jail awaiting trial. As his wife, Otha's girlfriend was then allowed to claim one of Otha's cars that had been impounded. Jack said he had found out later she had retrieved $60,000 in cash that had been hidden in that car. "He said, 'Man, I wish I had known that money was there,' and he looked at me. I just looked back like I was annoyed. I wasn't going to lead him on, but I knew he was feeling me out."

Hobbs noticed that Morrow was shaking so hard that his handcuffs were rattling. He wondered what Jack had said to him, how he had threatened him to scare him so much. The times Hobbs had talked to Morrow, he was very cool, couldn't be rattled. Everyone agreed that Morrow was going to try hard to make some cases for Hobbs and that Hobbs was going to try it a little longer before deciding to hand Morrow's case over to the feds. Attorney Greg Jones was waiting outside Jack's chambers and stood up as the meeting adjourned and everyone walked out. Jack put his hand on Greg's shoulder, looked at Hobbs, and then said to the young black attorney, "Be careful you don't drive on the wrong side of the road in Hoover, Jones. They don't like niggers down there."

Jack continued paging Hobbs to see how things were going. He asked the detective if he had heard of a drug dealer named Nate Jones. Yeah, Hobbs replied, he had heard of him. Jack said he had been hearing things about Nate Jones and wondered if Morrow could help Hobbs get him. "I want you to see if Morrow can get him" were Jack's words. Then Jack started telling Hobbs about his relationship with Warren King. He said that when he was a lawyer, he broke his leg and was laid up for some time. Warren King's father, Davis King, was a bail bondsman Jack knew, and he came to visit Jack in the hospital. Seeing that Jack was in financial straits, King had a number of his black clients come by the hospital and drop money on Jack's bed. When Jack thanked King, the bondsman said, "One day, you'll be a judge, and I'll need you." That's why he trusted Warren, Jack explained. At the time Davis supposedly did this, Jack was married to Sherry. When asked about Jack's story of Davis King's help, Sherry said she did not believe that it happened.

Hobbs reviewed the tape he had made of the meeting in Jack's chambers and then called McGregor and told him what he had. A few days later McGregor called Hobbs back and said, "Mark, I'm sorry, but you're going to be involved."

Hobbs then met with Brannan in the office of the Hoover police chief and turned over the tape. They talked over the options, and Brannan said the best thing to do was to turn Morrow over to the feds and try to get some cooperation out of him.

Giving up the case he and Doug had built against Morrow in exchange for catching a crooked judge seemed like a pretty good deal to Hobbs. The case was transferred, and Hobbs called Jack to let him know. Jack did not put up much of a fuss since Hobbs said it had already been done.

In early September 1992 Brannan interviewed Morrow in Hobbs's presence. They told Morrow they knew he was involved with Jack, King, and Greg Jones and that it would help his case if he helped them. "It kind of took the wind out of his sails," Hobbs said.

Morrow thought his case was still being taken care of and even assumed Hobbs was in on the scheme and getting part of the money. Morrow told Brannan everything he knew. He said the day after Hobbs arrested him, a friend visited him at the county jail and brought Greg Jones along. Morrow had never met Jones before, but his friend told him that Jones could do things for him that other lawyers, like John Robbins, could not.

When Morrow's wife, Sharice, who had already retained Robbins, visited Jones, he told her that he could guarantee that her husband would never go to prison, but it was going to take money. She went to Robbins's office and got back the $2,000 cash retainer she had given him. She then gave Jones $5,000 in cash. Later that night Jones visited Morrow again, this time with Warren King, who asked Morrow, "How much can you come up with?"

"What do you need?" Morrow asked.

"Can you come up with twelve?" King asked. Morrow said he could. "You can come up with the rest later," King said. "Twelve will be good for now."

The next day Robbins visited Morrow in jail and asked what was going on. Robbins said that he had gone to Judge Jack Montgomery to see about Morrow's bond but Jack was upset because Greg Jones, who was also claiming to be Morrow's attorney, had already visited him. Robbins said he would talk to Jack again in the morning.

That next morning, however, instead of lowering Morrow's bond after another visit from Robbins, Jack raised it to $500,000. Later that day Jones visited Morrow and told him not to worry, that the judge raised the bond just to rattle Robbins. He told Morrow that during his initial appearance in Jack's court, which would take place in a little while, the judge would do something to let him know he was on their side. That, Morrow said, was the first time he realized that part of this money was going into Jack's pocket.

A short while later Morrow was handcuffed to a few other prisoners and escorted into Jack's courtroom. When Jack walked in, the first thing he said was, "Who is Richard Morrow? I don't know what in the world you're doing here. They raided your house, find a little bit of marijuana, and then go thirty miles across town to an apartment that does not have anything to do with you and charge you with all of this cocaine."

Later Jack made a remark about Morrow having more lawyers than Noriega and sternly demanded, over and over again, to know who was representing him. Each time Morrow responded that Greg Jones was his lawyer. Later that day Jones met with Morrow in jail and told him that "all the cards were in place." He told Morrow he would be out of jail the next day and warned Morrow not to pay money to Warren King, to always pay him because he didn't trust King.

The next day Morrow was taken back to Jack's court for a bond hearing. That's when Jack put Morrow and Hobbs in his chambers and told them to talk things over a bit. When it was over, Jack lowered Morrow's bond. The judge again asked Morrow who was his lawyer. Morrow pointed to Greg Jones and said, "This man here." Later Warren King made the $25,000 bond for Morrow, and Morrow paid him $3,000 cash for the bond. While they were riding in King's car, King told Morrow that he needed the $12,000 now but that it was going to take a total of $35,000 to fix his case. Morrow said he could get the $12,000 by the next day at the latest. King responded, "Good. The man wants his money."

Morrow went to Greg Jones's house the next day and gave him $12,000 cash and another $5,000 in Western Union money orders that had been wired to him by his mother-in-law in California. Jones told Morrow to cash the money orders and bring back the cash, which Morrow did.

While Morrow was at Jones's house, a friend of Morrow's showed up to give Jones $1,500 that he had owed Morrow. Jones picked up the phone and called King. He told the bondsman that Morrow was there with him and that everything was fine. King talked to Morrow and told him to come by his house.

Morrow went to King's house later that day. King offered him a beer and then raised his shirt to show that he was not wired—Morrow did the same. King asked him how much money he had given Jones, and Morrow said $23,500 total. King said Jones had only turned over $14,500, and he got on the phone to call Jones and give him a hard time about not turning over all of the money. Jones said he just hadn't gotten around to it.

King then bragged to Morrow that he, and not Jones, was the one who made arrangements with Judge Jack Montgomery. He said his father used to do business with Jack. When his father died, King inherited the bonding business, and Jack came to him seeking the same arrangement he had with his father. Jack "sorta adopted" him, King said, and he called Jack "Dad."

To demonstrate his connection with Jack, King picked up the phone and dialed. He said into the receiver, "That guy we're working on is here right now. I want you to tell him who he needs to listen to." King handed the phone to Morrow, and a voice Morrow recognized as Jack's said, "Is this Morrow? How are you doing, young man?" Morrow said he was fine, and Jack said, "I hear you're getting a little confused about who to listen to. Listen to me very carefully. The only person you need to listen to is Warren King, your friend, who is sitting next to you."

A couple of weeks later, King and Morrow rode together to Jack's office for the meeting with Hobbs and his partner. After some discussion Morrow signed an informant agreement. After the officers left the room, Jack said, "Anytime you put a bunch of police together, they call themselves a task force and think they can do anything they want." Later King told Morrow that Jack was mad at Nate Jones because they had taken care of a case against him but he had not paid them the full $25,000 he owed them.

After hearing all of this, Brannan had Morrow set up with a wire and told him to arrange a meeting with Greg Jones. The two met on September 14 at the Carsmotology Car Wash. Brannan and DEA Agent Morris Moody were nearby, taking pictures of the meeting. Jones told Morrow that he had given all but $2,500 of Morrow's cash to Warren King. Both of them badmouthed King some, and Jones said, "I don't never give the judge shit because I don't want him to come back saying that I … you know. That's why I can't control what he does with the fucking money exactly. For all intents and purposes, he may have given the judge $2,500 or $5,000 of the money and is sitting on $17,000 and then act like he ain't got shit."

That meeting gave Brannan the corroboration of Morrow's story that he needed to get a court order for caller ID devices to be placed on Jack's and King's telephones so he could track who was calling whom. (Brannan didn't have enough probable cause for an actual wiretap yet. Besides, wiretap orders were only good for a certain number of days, and

Brannan did not think he was far enough along in the investigation for a tap to be useful.) Almost immediately, the ID devices showed that King and Jack were calling each other and that King and Greg Jones were calling each other.

On September 22 Morrow set up a meeting with King. "He was afraid King might pat him down because of what he did the time they met at King's house before," Brannan said. "So we had Morrow put on a jock strap, and we hid the wire in a cup. It was my old baseball cup."

Morrow went to King's house again, around 1:30 p.m. This time Brannan and Moody were not far away, watching the comings and goings. During that meeting King and Morrow badmouthed Greg Jones. King said he hadn't gotten any of the money Morrow gave to Jones, to which Morrow said that Jones had told him he gave King all but $2,500.

"That's a goddamn lie," King said. "When they raised your bond, Greg couldn't get it down. He came to me and told me you were going to pay so much to get it lowered. Now you know I ain't got none of that. So much and so much he gave me for the people who got it lowered down. This is what happened. The whole thing was, Greg told you right, you know. I couldn't tell you nothing else. They brought me in there and swore up and down they were going to do you right." King said he and Jack were mad at Jones, and they thought Morrow was part of the problem.

All of this was good corroboration and maybe even enough to get Jones and King on some kind of charge, but what Brannan really needed was a defendant who would make a deal and pay people in front of federal agents. He needed to catch the conspirators, especially the judge, in the act. He needed Nate Jones.

As if on cue, Nate Jones "flew in the window, out of the clear blue sky," Brannan said. "God wanted Jack Montgomery caught, that's all I could figure."

Actually Nate Jones's attorney contacted the U.S. Attorney's office. He said his client wanted to talk about a judge who was on the take. Word got to Brannan, and he anxiously volunteered to meet Nate Jones at a Shoney's restaurant in Anniston, Alabama, about halfway between Birmingham and Atlanta— where Nate Jones was living. There was no federal warrant out for Nate Jones's arrest, so Brannan was under no obligation to arrest him. Brannan and Nate Jones met on September 30 and talked for an hour. Nate Jones said he was willing to help and did not ask for anything in return, which Brannan thought was unusual.

Nate Jones told Brannan that he had known Greg Jones for some years. While he was a student at Cumberland Law School, Greg Jones used to work in a men's clothing store Nate Jones had owned on Birmingham's Southside.

In November 1991 Nate Jones was arrested in Shelby County, just south of Jefferson County, and charged with drug possession. He made bond and moved to Birmingham, where he was arrested several months later on a fugitive from justice warrant. Nate Jones was on Texas probation when Shelby County arrested him, and the arrest was tantamount to a probation violation—and Texas wanted him. While Nate Jones was in the Jefferson County jail on the Texas charge, awaiting possible extradition, Greg Jones visited him. Greg told Nate he could get a bond set for him, despite the no-bond order on the Texas charge, for $25,000. The money, Greg said, would be going to Judge Jack Montgomery, who was setting the bond.

Nate Jones's wife paid $10,000 to Greg Jones and Warren King. The next day Jack set Nate's bond at $5,000, and Nate walked out of jail on bond. He paid King another $5,000 but then skipped town for Atlanta before paying the last $10,000 of the bribe. About a month later, Jack placed a no-bond arrest order on Nate Jones's file, but that order could not reach across state lines.

After Nate Jones told him all of this, Brannan told Jones to call Warren King. When he did, a woman answered. He identified himself as Nate Jones, and the call was forwarded to another phone. King answered and said he was wondering when Nate Jones call. Nate responded that placing a no-bond on him was "fucked." King told him to simmer down—he would take care of that just as soon as Nate paid him the money he still owed. He told Nate to call him back the next day. The caller ID devices showed that Nate's call was forwarded to King's cellular phone.

Just a couple of minutes after Nate Jones and Warren King hung up, a call was made to Jack's house from a pay phone outside a drugstore.

The next day Nate Jones made a call from Atlanta to King at his favorite bowling alley. It was a conference call so Brannan could listen and record the call. King told Nate that his "folks" were mad at him because he still owed $11,000. He told Nate to give the money to a messenger he trusted and get it to Birmingham and they would take care of the no-bond and the extradition warrant out of Texas.

Brannan recruited FBI Agent Terry Fisher of Athens, Georgia, to come to Birmingham in a Porsche with Georgia license plates and act as the messenger. Brannan got $11,000 in cash, made a list of the serial numbers, and gave them to Fisher to deliver. Fisher went to King's house in the late afternoon of October 6, and Brannan and other agents watched as Fisher walked up to the door, introduced himself as Nate Jones's cousin, and went inside. Fisher left thirty minutes later without the $11,000. Thirty minutes after that, King climbed into his 1990 red-over-beige Lincoln Town Car with a license plate that said THE KING. Agents followed him as he drove to Jack's house after making a couple of quick stops. He stayed at Jack's for about an hour.

Brannan then requested and got a wiretap order and tapped Jack's telephone. King had told Nate that it was going to take more money to make the Texas case go away, and Nate agreed to pay $15,000 more. A payment of $10,000 was prepared the day after the first payoff was made. This time the cash was sprayed with a substance that only showed up under ultraviolet light. The spray, though, made the money feel strange. Brannan looked around the FBI office and spotted an empty doughnut bag that had powdered doughnuts in it. He put the cash inside and shook it up. The sugar might hinder the transfer of the spray substance, but at least the cash felt right.

FBI Agent Fisher went to King's house again and delivered him the marked bills. King got on the phone and called Jack. He told Jack he would come by that night, and Jack said he would take care of Nate's no-bond the next day. He also said he was going to try to get the Texas judge to transfer Nate's probation to Birmingham. Jack said he was even looking into the Shelby County case but that they were talking about giving the case to the feds. "But don't tell him about that yet," Jack told King. "Don't spook him yet." King hung up and told Nate's "cousin" (Fisher) about the bond being fixed in the morning. He also told him about Texas, but he didn't say a word about the Shelby case possibly going federal. King also said to tell Nate to watch out for Richard Morrow because he was a police informant.

Evidently these guys were playing twelve sides against the middle and back out again. It was amazing they kept it all straight, actually. Look at Morrow's bond: Jack jacked it up to $500,000 and then dropped it to $25,000. He told Hobbs he was doing that to make it clear to Morrow how important it was that he cooperate. Jones told Morrow that the judge did it to scare off Robbins. And it was at least implied to Morrow that it was a demonstration of how easily the strings could be pulled.

After Morrow was made an informant, Jack tried to get Hobbs to send him after Nate Jones. Why? Jack told Hobbs it was because he had heard bad things about Nate. In reality it was because Nate still owed money to King and Jack. The judge tried to use the cop and the informant as his own bounty hunters. When Nate went ahead and made things right, King essentially told Nate that Morrow might be after him. If that had happened in the real world, if Fisher really were Nate's cousin and Nate wasn't working with the FBI, that information could have been enough to get Morrow killed. There is very little honor among thieves.

After FBI Agent Fisher gave King the $10,000 payment, other FBI agents followed King as he drove it to Jack's house. King stayed at Jack's about two hours, and an hour or wo after he left, Brannan and Agent Alton Sizemore walked up to Jack's house and knocked on the door. Brannan had an eight-year-old wanted poster in his hand, just something he had grabbed at the office. Jack opened the door brandishing a short shotgun. He also had a .38-caliber pistol in his waistband and a .25-caliber in his pocket. Brannan introduced himself and the other agent and told Jack they were looking for a fugitive they thought might be in the area. He handed Jack the poster and asked him if he recognized the man. Jack took the poster, looked at it for a second, and said, "I've seen that guy. He was in my courtroom two weeks ago. I remember him because his girlfriend was there with him, and she had big tits."

It was all Brannan could do to keep from laughing. A normal human being would have looked at the poster and said, "Nope, never seen him before." Jack, though, could not resist making something up.

Jack went on to say that his sister had been an FBI agent some years ago but died under mysterious circumstances. They said it was suicide, Jack related, "but I've always wondered."

His sister, of course, was alive and well and not only had she never been an FBI agent—she hated FBI agents. When Brannan got the poster back to his office, he held it under an ultraviolet light, and one faint fingerprint showed up. The only way that could have happened was if Jack had at least touched the money that had been treated with the spray. They had him—now it was just a question of when to pounce.

Interestingly Jack actually called Brannan the next morning and asked him for a copy of the wanted poster Brannan had shown him at his house. Jack said he wanted to show it to his bailiffs and tell them to watch out for the fugitive. Brannan had already entered that poster, with Jack's glowing fingerprint on it, as evidence in the case against the judge—a key piece of evidence. So Brannan went scrambling around the FBI office, looking for another copy of the decoy poster. When he finally found one, he ran across Eighth Avenue North to Jack's courtroom—their offices were less than a block apart. Jack stopped the proceedings when he saw Brannan and made a big production out of receiving the poster and assuring the agent that they would watch out for this man. Brannan walked back to his office chuckling.

The feds went ahead and paid King his last $5,000, this time using Nate Jones himself to deliver the money. On October 20 Nate Jones and King met at a clothing store in Homewood, where they both had friends. Nate was wearing a wire, but the whole thing was a disaster. Employees kept coming up to him while he was wired and hitting him up for dope. Nate would say, "Not now, baby. This is not a good time."

Brannan and the other agents monitoring the wire just looked at each other and shook their heads. That wasn't exactly good evidence for the prosecution. Not only that, but King spent practically all of the $5,000 right there in the store. "We couldn't even retrieve it," Brannan said. "He had too many friends in there. They would have told him." That was money down the drain.

CHAPTER TWENTY-ONE

CAUGHT RED-HANDED

As Brannan prepared to get search warrants for Jack Montgomery's and Warren King's houses, the wiretaps stayed in place. Up until the last day, the taps continued to yield information not only about the known conspirators but also about people not yet on the playlist. Undercover conversations with King also included some hints that this thing had a broader scope than just the two drug dealers the investigation had been built upon.

At one point King told FBI Agent Terry Fisher that Nate Jones was getting off cheap. He said that one guy "had to get up $100,000 to get his shit straight." Another time King mentioned Jessie Struggs by name to Jones, saying they were charging Struggs $100,000.

Brannan checked into Struggs's record and saw that he had been busted that year by Tarrant police. Brannan talked to Tarrant Police Detective Warren Reno, who told Brannan that he had received a phone call from Judge Jack Montgomery shortly after he had put Struggs in jail for trafficking in cocaine. Jack had asked Reno if Struggs could be useful as an informant. Reno said he probably could be useful, but as of the time Brannan talked to Reno—four months after the arrest—Struggs had not given up the first piece of information. And Struggs's case had not yet received a preliminary hearing, which was very unusual.

After Brannan contacted him, Reno did some checking and learned that Struggs had been scheduled for a preliminary hearing in two weeks, with the notation on Struggs's record that no witnesses were needed—which indicated that Jack was planning to take a plea from Struggs on a reduced charge without telling anyone.

The wiretap on King's phone intercepted a call from Struggs in which the two agreed to meet at King's house. Surveillance at King's house witnessed Struggs driving up, getting out, taking something out of the trunk, and going into the house. Struggs stayed less than an hour, and King left about an hour after that and headed for Jack's place.

A couple of days later Reno called Jack to ask about the preliminary hearing and why there were no witnesses. Jack told Reno that the case against Struggs was weak and that he was trying to keep Reno from embarrassing himself in court. He said he would get Struggs to work on another case with Reno. The next day Jack called the assistant district attorney who was handling the Struggs case, criticized the evidence, and urged the prosecutor to settle the case at a lower charge with probation.

Also in undercover conversations King mentioned Ben Harrison and said that there were some things he was trying to do for Harrison. Brannan checked into the Harrison case and talked to DEA Agent Morris Moody about it. Moody told Brannan that he was handling the case because Birmingham Police Detective James Blanton had called and had asked him to take it over for him. Blanton said that after he had arrested Harrison, he started getting phone calls from Jack Montgomery asking him to make Harrison an informant in exchange for a reduced charge. Harrison never did any informant work, and Blanton turned the case over to the feds because he was afraid Jack would screw it up. Even if Brannan were not the wily, experienced agent that he was, he would have picked up on the pattern that was being exposed.

A few days before the wiretap was removed, agents intercepted a call to Jack Montgomery from "Tony," who told Jack that he had a new case to discuss with him and he'd come by the house in four minutes. About twenty minutes later agents heard Jack call the court clerk's office and ask about a new case against Antonio Stafford. Jack was told that there was no new case against Stafford showing in the computer yet but it would probably show up soon. Jack told them that when it did show up to assign it to his court.

Brannan found out that the narcotics detectives from the Jefferson County Sheriff's office had raided Stafford's house about a month earlier and seized cocaine and about $235,000 in cash from a safe, but Stafford hadn't been there. The detectives returned October 18, the day before the call from "Tony," seized more cocaine, and arrested Stafford, who was there this time. Brannan also found out that Stafford was being represented by Tony Falletta, a rather mousy but notorious defense attorney. In a much-publicized case in the late 1970s, Falletta had been charged and convicted of providing a gun to a convicted felon. He was disbarred for several years but had re-earned his license.

The day after Jack's meeting with Falletta, Nate Jones's last payment was delivered to King. That day King told Nate Jones that he had talked to "Dad" earlier in the day and that he now had to take care of Stafford. Agents who were following King watched him drive to a bar, where he met Stafford.

Around 2 p.m. October 22, Brannan was busy getting the search warrants ready to serve, when one more interesting phone call was intercepted. Attorney Jesse Shotts called Jack's house, and when Wendy answered the phone, Shotts asked, "Is your darlin' there?"

Wendy laughed and said, "Sure. But I warn you—he's in a mood."

When Jack got on the phone, Shotts asked if he would sign a bond on a defendant from another county. Jack balked a little and said he wasn't sure he could do that. Shotts said it would work with a sheriff's department stamp on it, which he could get later. Jack said he would try it. Shotts chuckled and said he had "5,000 reasons to try it."

Jack audibly perked up and said, "We'll take a chance … what the hell. Who gives a shit." Brannan listened to the tape of the call minutes later and was sorely tempted to try to catch Shotts in the act, but he had too many other things in motion with the search warrants.

Brannan got his search warrants at 4:55 p.m. from U.S. Magistrate Elizabeth Todd Campbell. At 7 p.m. Brannan and Agent Donna LeFebvre were standing on Jack Montgomery's doorstep. Wendy answered the door and invited the agents to come in. She told them that she and Jack had just finished dinner and made small talk about the World Series.

Jack greeted the agents heartily. As they all sat down in the living room, Jack said, "I've got lots of people going to the penitentiary tomorrow." The agents asked Wendy to leave the room and then started in by asking Jack about Morrow.

"Our drug people, the people on the task force, sat down with this guy," Brannan told Jack, "and he told them that he had paid a lot of money to his lawyer, Greg Jones, and that Jones told him that the money was being passed up the line somewhere."

Jack laughed and said, "I didn't get any of it, but I'm still waiting." He added that it wasn't unusual for a lawyer to overcharge a client by claiming he could pull strings with the prosecutor or even the judge.

When Brannan asked if Jack had ever heard of Warren King taking bribe money to fix cases, Jack said he hadn't. "I hear about cops taking bribe money," Jack said, "and I hear it about judges. I hear it about DAs, but I turned one of my DAs in. I caught one, and he went to the federal penitentiary. He stole from me, and you don't steal my sheets—you don't rig my cases without anybody knowing about it."

"Who was that?" Brannan asked.

"Lee Bragan," Jack replied. "I hope he dies of the bleeding piles. I'm not through with him yet." Jack then told Brannan the story of Davis King and how Davis had asked him to watch his son, Warren, and to take care of him.

"So you're that close to him then?" Brannan asked.

"Well, don't get me wrong," Jack said. "I know I'm still a judge and I've got ethical standards to uphold, but I turned him around. Now I don't know what he's doing when he's not around me, and he makes some serious-ass mistakes, but I try to lead him in the right direction. What he does with these flimflam jive-ass niggers of his doesn't concern me. That's his business. I don't ever go around that part of town."

Brannan used Jack's phone to call his supervisor and say loudly enough for Jack to hear, "We're finished up here."

But Brannan and LeFebvre continued to shoot the breeze with Jack, asking him about his background. At one point Brannan asked if the pension for a judge was any good. "Oh, Jesus, you wouldn't believe the retirement," Jack said. "I could walk off tomorrow if I wanted to, but I don't want to. I want to put in another eight years."

LeFebvre walked out to get Brannan's briefcase. When she returned, Agent George Moore was with her. At that point Brannan opened his briefcase and showed Jack the search warrant. As Assistant Special Agent in Charge Jim Carlile walked up to the house, it began to dawn on Jack that something serious was going on. Three more agents came in, and Brannan had Jack go around the house and gather and turn over all of his guns.

The agents found a total of $31,000 in cash squirreled away in several places. Of the $100 found in Wendy's wallet, all five $20 bills matched the serial numbers of the federal payoff money. Of the $509 found in Jack's wallet, five $20 bills also matched. Of the $25,950 found in the safe in the laundry room, which Jack voluntarily opened, 35 $1 bills, 161 $5 bills, and 7 $10 bills matched the serial numbers. None of the $1,500 found in a drawer in the bedroom closet or the $3,000 found in a kitchen drawer matched the serial numbers.

In searching Jack's house with ultraviolet light, the substance that had been sprayed onto the second payment to Warren King showed up in and around the safe, in the kitchen, on the dining room table, and on the TV remote control. Brannan had Jack Montgomery, and they both knew it.

CHAPTER TWENTY-TWO

I'm Scum Right Now

After Steve Brannan and the other federal agents had turned up the marked cash and the signs of the ultraviolet-sensitive spray in Jack Montgomery's house, Brannan escorted Jack back to his bedroom to sit down and talk where it was quiet. Here are some excerpts of Jack's conversation with Brannan and Donna LeFebvre.

Brannan: I think we got you, Judge.

Jack: I don't think so. I haven't done anything illegal. There's lots of money that comes through my wife's law practice.

Brannan: But you saw the fluorescent glow to that money—it was money that an FBI agent, undercover, gave to Warren King, and then we followed Warren over here to your house last Tuesday night and again last Wednesday night. So I know you couldn't have had that money for a long time.

Jack: OK.

Brannan: So my proposition, Judge, is that I've already told you we will not arrest you tonight.

Jack: OK.

Brannan: There are a lot of things you could tell us about lawyers paying people money to fix cases, about bail bondsmen paying money to fix cases, and I know that you're not the only one that's succumbed to temptation.

Jack: You know, I kept all this goddamn money right there, and I haven't spent a dime of it. I don't even know why I took it. It's not like me, but it's like getting a little bit pregnant, isn't it?

Brannan: Yes, sir. Yes, sir.

Jack: Eighteen years …

Brannan: I've heard a lot of good things about you. I've heard that you're a man who shoots from the hip and tells you what he thinks. I heard you had a hard time in Korea.

Jack: I've had a hard time everywhere I've been, and it's getting worse, and it's my own fault. It ain't nobody's fault but mine, and you know that. I mean, hell, I ain't bullshitting.

Brannan: The question is, what are you going to do now?

Jack: Well, I'm gonna do what you want me to do.

Brannan: OK, that's what I hoped to hear.

Jack: Well, I mean, it's obvious that you got me between a rock and a hard place.

Brannan: Yes, sir.

Jack: It's also obvious that I'm going to go through a lot of embarrassment, maybe.

Brannan: Well, we're not talking about being a snitch.

Jack: Well, that's what I'm going to be. Let's face it, pal, I'm scum right now. I know that and so do you, so let's don't kid ourselves.

Brannan: Well, I don't think it's that way, you know.

Jack: Are you serious? I just ruined everything I've worked for.

• • •

Brannan: Richard Morrow was in jail on a $250,000 bond.

Jack: Yeah.

Brannan: Then you raised his bond up to $500,000.

Jack: Yeah.

Brannan: And he had more lawyers than Noriega.

Jack: Yeah.

Brannan: And then, after him meeting with Hobbs in your chambers …

Jack: Yeah.

Brannan: … you lowered it to $25,000, and he made it with Warren King.

Jack: At the request of Mark Hobbs.

Brannan: OK. Any money change hands?

Jack: No.

Brannan: Well, Warren's holding out on you.

Jack: Well, I don't know. Now, see, that's the thing is— I don't know. He ain't holding out on me. We're not partners in this shit. We haven't done this except one or two times. I don't know how many times because sometimes it's been a little bit fuzzy.

Brannan: Yeah.

Jack: I can prove this medically, that at certain times of the day, I go a little nutsy.

Brannan. OK. And if while we're talking you don't feel good, if you need to take something, you be sure to let me know.

Jack: Oh, I will.

Brannan: You know, I don't want you going down on me here.

Jack: I'm not gonna have a fit on you.

Brannan: And I don't want you getting all depressed after we leave.

Jack: I'm not going to get all depressed after you leave.

• • •

Brannan: And I figure some of that money out there is from Jessie Struggs.

Jack: Well, that's something that I don't know that it would be or not. I don't think I've done nothing for Jessie Struggs. I've done nothing.

Brannan: Well, sir, I think you have.

Jack: What?

Brannan: I think you called the district attorney and persuaded him to offer Struggs a reduced charge from trafficking to possession.

Jack: If he helps.

Brannan: You said he's not going to do anything.

Jack: Well, I don't think he is either.

Brannan: Here's the way I see it, Judge. I have to go back and tell the U.S. Attorney that you admitted what we knew.

Jack: Yeah.

Brannan: And what we convinced you we could prove, and then beyond that, you just—I mean it's probably what I would do in your situation to tell you the truth—I would probably not want to admit any more.

Jack: But I didn't do anything with Struggs. Nothing's happened in the case.

Brannan: But did you take any money?

Jack: No, I don't think so. I swear to God I don't.

Brannan: And when Jessie took a package over to Warren and then Warren came out to see you.

Jack: I don't know anything about that.

Brannan: Well, I do because I saw it.

Jack: OK—but did you see him give me any money?

Brannan: No, sir.

Jack: OK—that's the thing about it. And I can't say that he did or he didn't because I was not in a real good frame of health at that particular time. I'd had some whiskey and it shot my sugar way down—it always does. And I may have taken some money— I may not have. I don't know anything about Jessie Struggs except that I read the DA's file, and it was a laugher. There's no witness in the case.

• • •

Brannan: Have you ever in your mind imagined what it would be like if something like this happened to you?

Jack: Sure, yeah, I did the first time I realized I'd just taken some money. But I've never taken money to fix a case.

Brannan: I think that's just a matter of definition.

Jack: Well, not with me it's not. I refuse to do that because I'm not going to fix a case and make something happen to the case. It comes in, and I know what's gonna happen to a case as soon as I look at the trial sheet.

Brannan: And you let them think that they're …

Jack: No, I don't let them think nothing. You're getting a massive thought plan right now. Forget that. This is just one guy I'm talking about. He says he's got this problem and so forth.

Brannan: Who's this—Warren?

Jack: Yeah. I don't like that kind of stuff.

Brannan: What kind of problem has he got?

Jack: I don't know. Too much drinking. I do too much drinking too, but that's not really an excuse. I don't know how much money is in that safe. I ain't got any idea how much is in there. Some of it has been in there for a long time. Some of it's been in there for a short time. I don't really think you're going to find any more.

Brannan: I noticed one thing in looking over the cases when allegations have been made against you …

Jack: Oh yeah, forever.

Brannan: … they're all drug cases—you've never been accused of having anything to do with a murder case or a rape case or anything like that.

Jack: Well, I'm glad. I didn't know that, but I'm, I'm glad. I'm not glad. This is the most sickening moment in my life. It really is [sigh]. But life goes on.

Brannan: Yes, sir.

Jack: Now, how do I go put these sons of bitches in the penitentiary tomorrow that I've got lined up to put in?

Brannan: Well, sir, if I were you, I wouldn't go down to the bench.

Jack: You would not?

Brannan: No, sir.

Jack: I can't just quit.

Brannan: You can go on leave.

Jack: How long you talking?

Brannan: Well, at least for a few weeks here. I mean, that's just what I would do. With this hanging over my head, I couldn't go down there and sentence somebody.

Jack: But I did not, have never—nobody's ever bought a case from me. OK?

Brannan: Well, sir …

Jack: I'm adamant about that.

• • •

[The phone rings.]

Jack: Hello? Yeah. Yeah, mmmmm. Yeah, I know. Yeah, I know.

Brannan: Warren?

Jack: Yeah [laughs]. Well, Warren, they're out here right now, and they're being very nice about it. They're not gonna haul my ass off tonight, but sooner or later I'll be gone. OK. Well, you stick to any story you want to. I got to go right now.

• • •

Brannan: OK, tell me one thing, Judge.

Jack: OK.

Brannan: When was the first time that Warren King came here and brought you a bundle of cash?

Jack: I do not know.

Brannan: I mean, has it been a year? Two years?

Jack: No, it hasn't been that long.

Brannan: This year?

Jack: Yeah. No—later part of last year, I believe.

Brannan: Latter part of last year?

Jack: Yeah. Something like that. Yeah. I'm not good at this.

Brannan: What?

Jack: I mean, this is not something I wanna remember. I wish I hadn't done it. I did it—that's that.

• • •

Brannan: You know you don't spend a lot of time at the office, so you need to do something at home.

Jack: No I don't. I sit here and drink. I don't go anywhere, don't do anything. When I go outside, I get in trouble. I got two people that want to kill my ass right now. How far away from your house would you go?

Brannan: Yeah, well, I saw in our files there'd been threats in the past—telephone threats that you'd received.

Jack: I've had five in my courtroom at the same time. Live killers.

Brannan: Yeah. How many years you been a judge?

Jack: Eighteen [sigh]. I'd like to retire and get out of here, but that's gone.

Brannan: Well, sir, it looks bad.

Jack: I know it does.

• • •

Jack: Well, listen, do you know what's going to happen to me?

LeFebvre: No, I don't know.

Jack: I'll tell you what's going to happen to me. I'm going to get indicted, and I'm going to be sent to a hard place. But I'll survive.

LeFebvre: I feel like that's a good possibility.

Jack: Oh, I can tell you that's what's going to happen. If the jury says I'm guilty, my ass is gone.

Brannan: I'm happy to leave it up to the jury about guilt, and I'm happy to leave it up to the judge for sentencing. I just try to do my job professionally and treat everybody with respect, even if they're a dope dealer or even if they're a white-collar criminal.

Jack: Is that what I am, a white-collar criminal?

Brannan: Mmm, it's more in what we would call public corruption.

Jack: Yeah, that's me. I'm a corrupt son of a bitch [laughs]. I can't believe this is happening to me. I mean, how can I do this to myself?

LeFebvre: Because people make bad choices all the time.

Jack: Yeah, I know.

LeFebvre: They do stupid things. But you have a lot to live for.

Jack: I don't have nothing.

CHAPTER TWENTY-THREE

NAKED AND BLEEDING

The day Jack Montgomery resigned from the bench, he went to see his lawyer, and then he called Brannan. He said, "I just resigned. I'm planning to plead guilty. I'm willing to cooperate against Warren King."

Brannan said something noncommittal and hung up. He didn't have the heart to tell the old guy that they didn't want his cooperation. Jack was the big fish, and they wanted other people to cooperate against him.

"At first Warren King denied everything," Brannan said. "He got a lawyer out of Atlanta, and the lawyer convinced him to do the best deal he could." Brannan met King at an Embassy Suites Hotel in January 1993, and the bail bondsman started to talk. He said the deal had been that he and Jack split all of the money fifty-fifty.

After his father, Davis King, died, the bonding business was shut down. Jack had helped Warren King by signing a bunch of blank bonds. That gave King an illegal but mostly risk-free way of doing some bond business. King could charge the client the normal bonding fee but with Jack's signature on the bond, King was not responsible for the surety. If the client skipped town and forfeited the bond, King was not liable for the amount of the bond. Warren was able to get Finley Avenue Bailbonds going again, and later Jack told him that he once had a money arrangement with a bondsman who had a fugitive out of Las Vegas and wondered if Warren wanted to try the same thing.

That's when it all started. The two started extorting money from a long list of defendants, mostly drug dealers, in exchange for lowered bonds or even guarantees of probation in exchange for guilty pleas. Jack had become his own criminal justice system, extracting "fines" from criminals and turning them loose.

Greg Jones heard about Jack and King's little system from one of his clients, King said, and wanted to get in on it. "He looks like a virgin to me," Jack said of Jones, but he allowed the young attorney to participate to a degree.

As King recounted client after client, he included Tony Scales, the drug dealer that Mayor Richard Arrington had been screaming about. He also talked about Nathaniel Allen, the man charged with murder, who Arrington later told the city council had been released on a bond that was far too low for the charge.

King then started talking about Morrow, not realizing that the investigation had started with Morrow. He said after the Hoover cop, Mark Hobbs, had transferred Morrow's case to the federal system, Morrow actually demanded his money back from King. To King that seemed impossible since he had already spent his share of Morrow's money, but he asked "Dad" about it anyway. "Screw him," Jack had told King. "Tell him the state case was dismissed like we said it would be. It's not our fault he landed in federal court."

Brannan took King's information and worked it for more than two months, talking to the defendants themselves, doing whatever he could to corroborate King's information. By March 10, 1993, the federal grand jury returned an impressive indictment charging Jack with one count of racketeering and four counts of extortion. The racketeering charge contained ten separate acts of bribery and extortion, involving ten separate defendants. King was also charged in the indictment with four counts of aiding and abetting Jack in extortion, and Greg Jones was charged with two counts of aiding and abetting.

On the day of the indictment Jack's attorney, Mark White, issued a press release that made it clear the defense would pursue the avenue that Jack himself started to pave on the night of the search warrant—he was too addled in the head by diabetes and alcohol to know what he was doing. "Since October 1992, Judge Jack Montgomery has been fortunate to be under the care of a team of caring physicians and health professionals," White's press release read. "The foremost concern since my assumption of Judge Montgomery's representation has been, and continues to be, Judge Montgomery's health. Judge Montgomery's organic brain impairment and resulting condition will be an issue before the federal court in these proceedings, and it would, therefore, be inappropriate for me to comment further regarding his condition.

"On behalf of Jack and his family, I would extend to the people of Birmingham heartfelt appreciation for the outpouring of expressions of concern for Jack's health over the past several months. These expressions of concern have been an important source of comfort to Jack. I would also express sincere appreciation for the prayers that have been offered for Jack and solicit them on a continuing basis."

Maybe Jack should be the one praying, was the comment heard in more than one newsroom as the press release was received on fax machines around town. Organic brain impairment? That sounded appropriately vague, reporters murmured. Who doesn't suffer from organic impairment? Hell, it's probably a requirement for city editors.

Specific or not, it was clear that the defense was going to say Jack was nuts. Of course everyone had been saying that for years, but White had to prove it medically and legally. One couldn't help but recall a quote of Jack's from several years earlier: "You see, one thing I don't like is certain individuals who try to work the system to their advantage, like defendants. I know all their tricks—I invented half of 'em."

Jack's case had been assigned from the start to Assistant U.S. Attorney Mike Rasmussen, a tireless, no-nonsense prosecutor whose calm demeanor and capacity for detail were perfectly suited to the rigid requirements of federal court and specifically the mind-numbing thoroughness demanded in public corruption cases. He was a military brat, born in Hawaii. His father, Philip Rasmussen, was one of seven American pilots who were able to get their planes in the air during the attack on Pearl Harbor, and he shot down a Japanese plane before landing his own plane with more than 600 bullet holes in it. Mike and his family had lived in Albuquerque, Tehran, and Istanbul. He loved seeing the world, but he also grew up isolated and lonely. Mike was interested in a military career, but it was the end of Vietnam and the ranks were being downsized. Besides, like Brannan, his eyesight was not good enough to be a pilot. So he entered Cumberland Law School, where he graduated in December 1975.

Rasmussen started his career in the Jefferson County District Attorney's office and then moved to the U.S. Attorney's office in 1978. He had a special distaste for corrupt officials and had more than his share of those cases to prosecute, beginning with the sheriff of Marshall County, who took a bribe from bootleggers. He had heard things about Jack Montgomery for years. When the case was assigned to him and he got into it, he admitted that it "irritated" him even more that Jack falsely claimed he was a POW. "It cheapens what real heroes do," said the son of the World War II fighter pilot who was awarded two silver stars.

Within a day or two of the indictment, Mark White, Jack's attorney, filed a motion seeking to have Jack declared incompetent to stand trial. His client had been unable to assist in his own defense, White claimed. The prosecution countered with a motion to have Jack placed in federal custody to be examined by psychologists. White then requested that Jack be examined in Birmingham so as not to threaten his health any further.

A hearing was held before U.S. Magistrate Paul W. Greene to determine where to put Jack, and the defense called Dr. Buris Boshell to the stand. Boshell was one of the country's leading endocrinologists and an expert on the treatment of diabetes.

Boshell had diagnosed and treated Jack after he fell down the stairs in 1972. In fact Jack's wife at the time, Sherry, credited Boshell with saving Jack's life after the fiasco at the first hospital where Jack had been treated. The next time Boshell saw Jack was twenty years later, about a month after his resignation. The doctor testified that Jack Montgomery was "dancing on the razor's edge" mentally and physically and that placing him in a federal prison's hospital could cause him to "be potentially suicidal or go into complete psychosis. He has had extensive brain cell loss."

It also came out in the hearing that Jack had been abusing the Xanax that had been prescribed to him for what had been diagnosed as post-traumatic stress disorder stemming from his experience as a POW. And in the last couple of years, Jack had been taking anabolic steroids in an attempt to regain some sexual vigor for the sake of his much younger wife.

Greene said he did not see the difference between turning Jack over to the Bureau of Prisons or keeping him in Birmingham and ruled that Jack would be examined at a prison facility. However the magistrate reversed himself the next day and ordered Jack to report to Brookwood Hospital in Birmingham for fifteen to twenty-five days of mental evaluation.

By that time Jack's drug regimen included Isosorbide, Procardia XL, Lopressor, Dyazide, Proscar, aspirin, ibuprofen, and Relafen—most of which were for his high blood pressure and regulation of his heart. Doctors seemed to agree that the magnetic response imaging of Jack's brain showed decreased activity, but they differed on whether or not it was a level to be expected for a man of his age. They also thought there were signs of damage done to the brain as in the case of small strokes, but Jack had never had a diagnosed stroke.

The cases against Jack and the other two defendants were then assigned to U.S. District Judge Sharon Lovelace Blackburn. For those who knew Jack and had been following the case, this may have been the ultimate irony. Jack hadn't simply drawn a woman to hear his case, which almost certainly galled him—he drew the first and only woman on a federal bench in the state. Blackburn was a 1977 graduate of Cumberland Law School, where Jack had earned his degree.

Blackburn was not what one expected of the average federal judge—she was young and attractive with jet black hair and blue eyes. She was so attractive that the U.S. Senators who approved her nomination in 1991 nearly put their feet in it. Alabama's own Howell Heflin commented that lawyers and defendants in Blackburn's court "won't be able to take their eyes off the bench." Strom Thurmond of South Carolina later said her looks "didn't hurt her nomination." U.S. Representative Sonny Callahan of Mobile, Alabama, who was testifying on Blackburn's behalf, responded, "They say beauty is only skin deep—but so is ugly. It doesn't hurt to have a pretty one." The comments by the old boys brought the expected reprimand from the National Organization of Women, and Blackburn's nomination sailed through.

That is not to say that Blackburn was not qualified. She served in the U.S. Attorney's office for twelve years—six in the civil division, followed by six in criminal. She came from a family of lawyers on her father's side and a family of politicians on her mother's, including her uncle, one-time U.S. Postmaster General Winton M. "Red" Blount.

When Jack drew her as his judge, the prosecution was secretly thrilled. Since so much of the defense's incompetency argument was going to center around Jack's diabetes, the prosecution thought it was a plus that Blackburn was thoroughly familiar with the disease since her husband was an insulin-dependent diabetic.

Jack was obviously less than thrilled with being judged by this forty-three-year-old woman, and every once in a while he allowed the judge to see his disdain. If she had been in his court-room, he probably would have swatted her on the behind.

The competency hearing began in mid-June 1993. And while the defense said it intended to prove that Jack's condition had rapidly deteriorated since the beginning of his last year on the bench, Rasmussen said he intended to prove that not only was Jack competent to stand trial but also that he had been attempting to fake symptoms of mental defect.

"Malingering" the doctors called it. Baltimore forensics psychiatrist Jeffrey Janofsky testified that at one point in his interview with Jack, the exjudge said he could not remember if he had any children. "I've treated hundreds, maybe thousands, of patients," Janofsky testified. "When someone gets to the point where they truly can't remember if they have any children, they are drooling in bed and incapable of doing anything for them-selves. That's not the case here."

Janofsky also pointed out that when he asked Jack what the date was that day, he said it was the 14th, when in fact it was the 15th, and he did that without looking at the calendar on his own watch. "I think that was a case of deliberately giving a wrong answer," he testified.

Outside the courtroom, Mark White, Jack's attorney, told reporters, "I'm afraid to look at my watch in front of this guy."

Sherry came up from her home in Mobile to testify about the acts of violence Jack committed against her while they were married, and bailiff Chris Galbaugh testified that the judge was getting more difficult to handle during his last year. "There were times when he'd be speaking to defendants who were brought into the courtroom in shackles," Galbaugh said, "and if one of them said something he didn't like, he'd get right in that person's face and start screaming."

Rasmussen called Art Spears, a dog breeder and trainer from Shelby County, to the stand and had him testify about the couple of phone calls he had received from Jack just two months earlier. Jack had been looking for a dog for Wendy, Spears said. He seemed to have a clear mind and to be capable of carrying on a conversation about dogs.

Another forensic psychiatrist, William Grant, testified that he found Jack capable of understanding the charges against him and aiding in his defense. "There was no evidence of thought process disorder, hallucinations, or delusions," Grant said. "Jack insisted that he had never taken a bribe for fixing a case, and he said he thought he was going to get out of it."

There was also testimony that Jack had done strange things at Brookwood Hospital such as taking his ice bucket to the ice machine and hitting the button for ice while holding the bucket upside down. It was all starting to have a *One Flew Over the Cuckoo's Nest* feel to it.

White later told reporters that "incompetence is not a defense of choice." It may not have been his defense of choice, but the prosecution was contending that it was Jack's defense of choice. If he was found incompetent, he would be placed in a secure medical facility until he was competent, at which point he would be tried.

At the end of the three-day hearing, Judge Blackburn said she would issue her ruling in a week or so. Just before Blackburn was to issue her ruling on Jack's competency to stand trial, something happened that would have made some people second-guess such a decision. That may actually have been the plan.

Friday afternoon, July 9, 1993, someone called the Vestavia Hills Police Department and reported a man down on the side of the road in the 2600 block of winding Rocky Ridge Road. Officer Greg Lee was dispatched to check things out. A few minutes after 3 p.m., he spotted a naked man lying at the bottom of Jack's steep driveway and a couple of passersby who had stopped to help him. Officer Lee could see right away that the man had a cut on his forehead and some abrasions on his arms and legs. The man was dazed and could not tell the officer who he was or what happened. It didn't take Lee long, however, to figure out that the incoherent naked man was Jack Montgomery.

One passerby, Keith Roberts, told Lee he saw Jack running down his driveway stark naked before he tripped and fell. Another passerby, Jimmy Plott, was on his way home from work when he saw Jack sitting at the bottom of the driveway, obviously in pain. "Someone brought him a towel," Plott said, "and he just threw it away. I said, 'Hey, man, nobody wants to look at you naked.' But he wouldn't listen."

Plott didn't know the man was Jack Montgomery until later that day. He asked the man questions, but all Jack answered was "I don't know," even when Plott asked him who he was. "I felt like I had seen him before. He looked up at me with the clearest blue eyes I ever saw. I don't think I'll ever forget those eyes."

As the paramedics who had answered the police call worked on Jack, Lee and another officer walked up to Jack's house. The garage door was standing open, and they walked into the house and found no one else inside. Jack was taken to Brookwood Hospital, where doctors determined that he had broken his hip. On the way to the hospital, the paramedics discovered that his blood-sugar level was quite low, registering thirty-seven. That level, Dr. Boshell said later, could only be produced by an overdose of insulin or an extreme lack of food, perhaps combined with too much strenuous exercise.

The day after the incident, Jack's attorney, Mark White released a statement saying that Jack had been taking a shower when he suffered a bout of hypoglycemia, fell, broke his hip, then crawled down the driveway for help. Officer Lee had already thought of that. He had checked the shower when he went into the house that day—it was not running, and the tub was not wet. There was no blood in the bathroom or any other indications in the house that something was wrong. And he had already noticed that Jack's hair was not wet.

The media replayed details of the bizarre incident, becoming openly fascinated with all the twists and turns developing in the case. The phrase forever after used in reference to that day was "naked and bleeding," as in "you'll remember July 9 when Jack Montgomery was found naked and bleeding in his driveway."

As if things weren't weird enough, the doctors sent Jack home from the hospital after two weeks. Three days after he got home, he called the Vestavia Hills police and told them that he remembered what had really happened that day. He said he'd been swimming in his pool that morning and then went inside to take a shower. He heard a knock at the door, and when he answered the door, he saw four men dressed in suits and ties. Three of the men pulled him outside and beat him with their fists and rocks they found in the yard. The fourth man, who appeared to be the leader, stood and watched. Then the men drove off in a black Crown Victoria.

Jack said he did not recognize any of the men and they didn't say a word to him. When a *Birmingham News* reporter called Jack at home about this latest development, the exjudge said the events of that day were "coming back to him in bits and pieces."

It was too late, though. Judge Blackburn had already declared him to be competent to stand trial—whenever that was going to be.

Nobody was buying the four men in the suits either. Even White could not bring himself to exhort the police to broadcast lookout reports for the black Crown Victoria. Instead he notified the court that the defense planned to employ an insanity defense once his client was physically able to stand trial. The incident itself raised some interesting questions and even more interesting possible questions: Jack's blood sugar had fallen to a very low level. Did he let that happen on purpose? Did he even induce it? Being naked outside was a wonderful touch if someone was trying to convince others that he was crazy. It certainly didn't seem like he had been taking a shower anytime recently. Why was he running down the driveway? Was he going to flag someone down for help? Why not simply call the paramedics? Maybe he simply planned to take a little naked jog up the road in front of the schoolkids coming home, knowing the police would pick him up. If he were caught jogging naked, people would have to say he was crazy. There was one other possibility—Jack intended to run into the middle of traffic and end it all. No one will ever know what was in his mind at that time or how addled his mind was with the effects of hypoglycemia.

The U.S. Attorney's office, after Brannan had investigated the incident, opted to believe that Jack meant to hurt himself. No one thought he meant to break his hip, but Rasmussen believed it was just another delaying tactic. He filed a motion asking Blackburn to revoke Jack's bail and place him in a Bureau of Prisons hospital facility or the psych ward at Brookwood Hospital. He enumerated his reasons:

—Evidence before the court has shown that the defendant has a history not only disregarding his health needs but of willfully abusing his health.

—Evidence before the court has shown that the defendant is antisocial and has a disregard for social norms.

—Evidence before the court has shown that the defendant is a malingerer.

—Evidence before the court has shown that the defendant, a former judge, is depressed, probably due to the stress of the proceedings against him.

—There is evidence before the court that the defendant has expressed thoughts of suicide.

—Evidence, in the form of tape recordings and search warrant affidavits before the court, has shown that the case against the defendant is strong.

—It is to the defendant's advantage to obstruct and delay the proceedings against him.

"It is apparent from the foregoing that the defendant has and will continue to engage in self-destructive behavior with the effect, if not the intention, of obstructing the proceedings against him. Hospitalization under controlled circumstances is the only way of guaranteeing his timely appearance at trial."

White scoffed at the motion, saying, "I've got better things to do with my time than to respond to something as silly as this. This is the first time I've ever heard of incarcerating someone because he broke his hip. What would they have done if he'd broken his legs—tried to execute him?" Judge Blackburn denied the motion to revoke bond, but she did appoint Wendy to be her husband's twenty-four-hour-a-day custodian, ordering her not to leave him except when absolutely necessary.

In late November a hearing was held to determine when Jack would be physically able to stand trial. Wendy took the stand and testified that "he's so weak at this point that when he gets dressed, he has to sit down a lot. It's a piecemeal operation and can take about an hour." She said he spent most of his days in bed but did walk around with crutches a little.

"Has he had any alcohol?" Rasmussen asked her.

"Nope," she said.

The hearing was moved into Blackburn's chambers to hear telephone testimony from Jack's orthopedic surgeon, Dr. Perry Savage. Under questioning, Savage said that Jack was healing well but was still complaining of pain, perhaps more than he should be. He also pointed out, with some dismay, that a physical therapist had recently stopped going to Jack's home because he was constantly complaining and refusing to do the movements she told him to do.

When Savage was asked about the date that was being considered for trial, January 3, he said he thought Jack should be sufficiently healed by then. "I think he'll still complain of some pain," Savage said. "You may need a soft, comfortable chair for him, one that can lean back. And take some breaks every couple of hours to let him stretch. Otherwise he should be fine."

While still in chambers, Rasmussen pointed out to Judge Blackburn that just a week earlier, Wendy had to call paramedics to the house to revive Jack from unconsciousness due to low blood-sugar level. He said he was still concerned that something would happen to Jack between then and the trial date and once again asked Blackburn to consider his motion to place Jack in custody. Blackburn also said she was worried about that.

At that point Wendy with tears running down her face, raised her voice at Blackburn and said, "I take care of him as good as anybody could, and it's not up to you to take that away from me." When she finished she just looked down and sobbed. A moment later White said in a quiet tone, "Judge, this is a young woman who has been a custodian for months under very trying circumstances. To be his custodian twenty-four hours a day is not an easy job."

With that said, it seemed strange that the defense was asking for the situation to continue, putting further stress on Wendy—stranger still that Blackburn again denied the prosecution's motion and ordered Wendy to closely monitor Jack's food and insulin to prevent any further bouts of hypoglycemia.

CHAPTER TWENTY-FOUR

A PLEA

Of the three indicted coconspirators, Attorney Gregory DeWayne Jones was the first to be put on trial. It was clear from the start that Jones was a minor player in this scheme. He was just a young man who wanted in on a good deal—and greed got the best of him. Instead of reporting Jack Montgomery and Warren King, he wanted a piece of the action.

For Rasmussen and Brannan, the Jones trial was a dress rehearsal for the upcoming Jack Montgomery trial. A couple of days earlier, King had showed up for his trial date but had changed his not-guilty plea to guilty. If anyone didn't know it before, they knew then that King was going to testify against Jones and Jack.

A tall, thin black man of thirty-two, Jones looked like a deer caught in the headlights that day in September 1992 in Judge Blackburn's court. Facing two counts of aiding and abetting extortion, Jones was obviously frightened of what would happen to him. Would he be sent to prison? Probably. Would he lose his license to practice law? Almost certainly.

Jones was represented by Bill Clark, one of the most capable attorneys in town. A square-jawed ex-military man who spoke in forceful tones, Clark had represented some of the state's most celebrated defendants over the years, including ousted Governor Guy Hunt. He was just about the best defense that money could buy, but he didn't have much to work with in the Jones case. It was evident that he wasn't going to let anything slide by though.

After the jury of thirteen women and one man was selected, Clark made three separate motions for dismissal, all based on the way the jury was selected. All three were denied, but Clark wasn't going to stop swinging. In his opening statement to the jury, Clark said that whatever King and Jack had cooked up, Greg Jones was not involved. He wasn't paid anything that he shouldn't have been paid, and Greg Jones never gave any money to Jack, Clark said.

Rasmussen called the elusive Nate Jones to the stand. Shelby County still wanted Nate Jones on a drug charge, but he was living in Atlanta, and only the feds could get their hands on him. Nate Jones strode in, settled into the witness stand, and proceeded to tell the jury how Greg Jones came to see him in the county jail. Nate said he complained to Greg that Jack wouldn't set a low enough bond for him to get out. "Greg Jones said, 'Well, Jack just wants to get paid.' " Greg Jones later brought King to see Nate, and they told him that they could get him out for $25,000.

Nate's exwife, Beverly Creagh, testified that when she delivered $10,000 in a paper bag to Greg Jones and Warren King at a nightclub, Greg told her that "he was going to take the money to Judge Montgomery, and he'd set bond, and Nate would be out before the night was out." She said that when she asked Greg how she could be sure that he wasn't just pocketing the money, he told her that ten grand was "chump change" and that her husband was still going to have to come up with more money once he was out of jail.

As the trial went on, the prosecution presented much of its case against Jack Montgomery, at times not even mentioning Greg Jones. Rasmussen contended that he had to lay the groundwork of the Montgomery case in order to show how Greg was an active go-between on two occasions. Clark, however, objected twenty times in one day as Rasmussen continued that strategy.

The trial stalled several times when Blackburn called the attorneys to her chambers to discuss Clark's objections, and she did overrule almost all of them. Rasmussen would call a witness, get him to tell his part of the Jack Montgomery scheme and then sit down. Clark was left to simply ask each of them, "Did you see Greg Jones during this time? Did the name Greg Jones ever come up?"

Clark did his best to discredit Nate Jones when he took the witness stand. He asked him detailed questions about all of the criminal cases pending against him. He also asked Nate over and over what the government had promised him in exchange for his testimony. Nate kept saying, "Nothin'." Finally Clark asked, "You would lie about Greg Jones to stay out of jail, wouldn't you?"

"No," Nate Jones said. "I'm not in a position where I have to lie."

The prosecution called Warren King to the stand. Warren sat there, wearing enough gold jewelry to be Mr. T's brother-in-law, and laid the whole thing out for the jury. "I had a miserable time trying to run the business," he said. "Jack Montgomery told me that my father had told him to look after me, to take care of me." The extortion scheme, he said, was the judge's idea. "Jack told me I wasn't doing nothing illegal." Not only that, he said, but Jack also forced him to take part in the extortions. He "told me that if he didn't approve a bond for me, I wouldn't make any money. I had no choice if I wanted to keep my business."

King said Jack called him periodically to see if he had any new prospects, defendants who would be willing to pay for judicial favors. One guy, Jomo Mitchell, had a drug charge on him, King said, and kept fretting about the case. "Jomo worried me for about three weeks. I told him, 'Jomo, you've got nothing to worry about. You've got a good lawyer and a good case,' but he wanted a guarantee. When Judge Montgomery asked me if I had anybody, I told him about Jomo, and he said, 'If he wants to give money, let him give it.' "

King also made it clear that Greg Jones was not the fringe player he might have appeared to be. "Greg didn't need me to deal with Dad," he testified. At one point in the Richard Morrow case, King testified, Greg called King to his law office, gave him $7,000 he said came from Morrow, and told him to take it to Jack Montgomery.

Morrow's wife, Sharice, testified that she first met Greg Jones at the jail. She said he started telling her that he and no one else could get her husband out of jail. He said the lawyer she had hired wasn't any good. "Gregory Jones said that he and the judge were real close," Mrs. Morrow said.

Attorney John Robbins, the one Mrs. Morrow had hired, testified about his meeting with Jack to see about reducing Morrow's bond. Jack had asked Robbins if Morrow had paid him a retainer. When Robbins said he had not, Jack had said that, "I wasn't his lawyer until I'd been paid." After Mrs. Morrow gave Robbins the $3,000 retainer, Robbins went back to Jack. Robbins tesified that Jack seemed upset when Robbins told him he had received a retainer and said Morrow "was jerking him around" and that he "needed to get more information." That's when Jack raised Morrow's bond to $500,000.

Morrow later testified that Greg Jones had told him that "he could work some special services and could do things my regular lawyer couldn't do. He told me he could pay the judge." Morrow also told the jury about Greg Jones and King arguing back and forth about how Morrow should not trust the other. Rasmussen played the tape of Morrow talking to Jones at the car wash.

Sergeant Mark Hobbs testified about how Jack had tried to turn Morrow into an informant. "The whole thing was unbelievable," Hobbs said on the stand. "I never had anything like this happen with a judge before. I felt something was wrong. I felt there might be something illegal going on."

The defense did the only thing it could do—it put Greg Jones on the stand, and Jones did his best to quite simply deny everything. On cross-examination, Rasmussen practically shouted at Greg, "Are you telling this jury that you had no idea Mr. King was taking money to Judge Montgomery?"

"No, I did not," Greg Jones replied, almost sheepishly.

When asked about Nate Jones, Greg explained that he was never Nate's attorney of record and that he had only been talking to Nate as a friend. "I didn't make any guarantees," Greg testified.

About Morrow, Greg Jones simply said, "I didn't really want to represent Richard Morrow." All of the cash that Morrow gave him, Greg said, he gave to King as payment for making Morrow's bond. He said he had no idea that Morrow supposedly had a deal with King and Jack Montgomery until Morrow's case was transferred to federal court and Morrow told him. Greg said he promised to help Morrow get some of his money back from them.

Rasmussen played a tape of a telephone conversation between Greg Jones and Morrow. Greg was heard to say, "I went by to see our other buddy, and he had gone for the day. But I'll find him and let him know what the deal is."

Greg Jones admitted on the stand that the "other buddy" was Jack, but, he said, "I was telling Morrow that I was going to confront Warren King and confront Jack Montgomery with what he told me and help him get his money back."

Greg Jones's denials were as effective as a chicken-wire umbrella. The jury wasn't buying it. "The evidence in this case isn't even close. It's overwhelming," Rasmussen said in his closing statement. "It all adds up to the guilt of Greg Jones."

Throughout the prosecution's summation, Greg Jones sat at the defense table and simply shook his head "no" over and over again. In his closing, Clark attacked the credibility of the witnesses. He said they were all lying in order to make their own legal problems disappear. But the jury agreed with Rasmussen and returned a verdict of guilty on both counts in just three hours.

The Rasmussen-Brannan juggernaut had a full head of steam and was chugging straight for Jack Montgomery. In her instructions to the Greg Jones jury, Blackburn told the jurors that they had to find that Jack Montgomery had taken bribes in order to find Greg Jones guilty of aiding and abetting the crime. The fact that the jury came to that conclusion so quickly meant impending doom for Jack.

Monday, January 3, arrived and Jack Montgomery didn't. After all that had happened over the last year, nobody really seemed that surprised. Defense Attorney Mark White informed Judge Blackburn that Jack had suffered another episode of hypoglycemia that morning. He was reportedly semiconscious and incoherent, and Wendy called an ambulance to the house. When these episodes had happened a few years ago, one of Jack's bailiffs would have simply brought him a Coke and things would have moved right along. Would Jack make it to court today? Blackburn wanted to know. Hopefully after lunch, White replied.

The truly weird news was that Jack, who was still supposedly all but bedridden from his broken hip, had cut himself across the gut with a chain-saw Saturday. White explained that Jack had been walking in his yard because they had all been after him to get some exercise. He had spotted a chain saw that had been left on the ground by a tree trimmer who was taking a break. "I don't know exactly what he did, but he started up the chain saw, and it cut him," said White.

Apparently the cut looked worse than it was, but everyone in the courthouse was certainly wondering if this was another attempt by the cagey old guy to delay things just one more time.

Could Jack Montgomery really have aimed a roaring chain saw at his own gut? Reporters shuddered as they discussed the possibility. Anyone who would do that might be crazy after all, they said.

Just before noon, Jack and Wendy showed up at the federal courthouse. Jack was on crutches and seemed alert and strong. He didn't say anything as the reporters outside of the courthouse threw a few questions at him. In the courtroom, Rasmussen again pleaded with Judge Blackburn to place Jack in some kind of federal custody. Between the chain-saw incident and that morning's low blood-sugar level attack, Rasmussen said, the government was confident that Jack would do anything to himself to delay trial further.

The rest of the day was spent in closed-door meetings with the judge and attorneys. A rumor started that there was a plea in the air. When the press caught up with the attorneys from both sides, White said he could not respond to questions about a plea and Rasmussen would only say that no plea offer, no reduced sentence in exchange for a guilty plea, had been offered to the defense. Blackburn ended the day by saying the motion to revoke Jack's bond was still under consideration and that court would resume at nine o'clock the next morning.

On Tuesday Jack actually showed up on time. After a short meeting in back rooms, everyone filed into the courtroom. Attorney Al Bowen, an experienced old codger who had been riding shotgun with White throughout the case, stood up and told Blackburn that the defense now wished to change its plea of not guilty to what was known as an Alford plea. In this best-interest plea, Bowen said in court, the defense merely acknowledged that the prosecution had a case that was strong enough to virtually guarantee a guilty verdict. It was more or less a no-contest plea with some picky legal differences.

White later said that he did not know Jack was considering a plea until Monday. "He looked at me and said, 'I want to plead. I don't think I can make it through a trial.' " Despite the rumors of the day before, the reporters who were covering the trial seemed surprised at the plea and momentarily confused by its complexity. Most had been betting that Jack was not going to go down without a fight.

Rasmussen and Brannan did not look elated. They knew that the real value of this whole case was putting it out in the open, letting the public see day after day with testimony from live witnesses and displays of color glossy photos just how corrupt Jack Montgomery had been. The Slamming Judge, the law-and-order guy who wouldn't stand for legal maneuvering and shenanigans in his own courtroom had taken the weasel's way out. Jack Montgomery had prevented the case from being heard in its entirety, and for the record, he did not have to admit his guilt.

In order for Blackburn to accept the plea, however, Rasmussen did have to present her with a summary of the case that he would have put on. For several hours, Rasmussen went through the thirty-five witnesses he intended to call and what he expected them to say. He entered seventy exhibits as evidence. Anyone could see that his heart wasn't in it though. All of the work he and Brannan put into the case would go all but unnoticed and unappreciated.

After Rasmussen was through with his presentation, Blackburn asked Jack a few questions, such as did he understand the plea that had been entered for him. Jack answered all of her questions with a simple "Yes, ma'am" or "No, ma'am."

Jack faced a possible maximum sentence of one hundred years in prison and $1.25 million in fines. U.S. Attorney Claude Harris stood outside the courthouse and told reporters, "We're going to insist on an upper-range sentence. We feel very strongly about this case. The only thing worse than a crooked prosecutor is a crooked judge. It strikes at the very core of our judicial system."

Sometime later *The Birmingham News* printed an editorial with the headline "Judge not: Jack Montgomery's case a triumph of games over justice." The newspaper article said, "Mind you, he didn't actually say he was guilty—nothing that remorseful— just that the overwhelming amount of evidence indicated that he was. And it did. Assistant U.S. Attorney Mike Rasmussen proceeded with almost a four-hour recitation of the evidence against Montgomery. It would be a stiff challenge to catch someone more red-handed."

Rasmussen once again asked Blackburn to revoke Jack's bond and place him in federal custody. She denied the motion and continued with Wendy acting as Jack's custodian. Blackburn set the sentencing date for Valentine's Day, a little more than a month away. Asked by a reporter at the end of the proceedings if he was worried about Jack's health or what he might do to himself, Defense Attorney White said simply, "I worry about him everyday."

CHAPTER TWENTY-FIVE

CLEARED BY A BULLET

When Wendy left the house about 5:30 Saturday evening, February 12, 1994, she was just running out to the grocery store, she told police. When she left, Jack was sitting on the bed watching TV. In two days Jack was supposed to appear in federal court to be sentenced.

The defense had asserted that it believed the sentence should be between thirty-three and forty-one months, but that was just wishful thinking. Judges were not given minimal sentences for corruption. They knew that. When Wendy returned to the house after an hour, maybe more, Jack was nowhere to be found. Frantic, she called Vestavia Hills Police Captain Calvin Williams and said her husband was missing. After she made the call, she grabbed a flashlight and went searching through their neighbor's backyard.

Corporal Tim Holcomb and Officers Jeff Stewart and Wayne Anderson were dispatched to Jack's home. They arrived a minute or two after 7 p.m. and found the door from the carport open. Inside, they found Wendy sitting on the living room floor sobbing. She said she had found Jack in the basement. All she saw with her flashlight were his legs, but they weren't moving. She led the officers to the door outside that went down to the basement. No lights were on, so the officers pulled out their flashlights and went in. They entered the part of the basement where the furnace and hot water heater sat. And there was Jack, lying on his left side by the water heater. He wasn't moving, and there was a visible wound in the center of his chest. His glasses were on the floor near the lower part of his right leg. He was wearing a blue terry-cloth shirt, gray sweatpants, blue socks, and Docksiders. Water was spewing from a broken valve on the water heater, and a large puddle surrounded Jack's body. Investigators figured that Jack fell, hit the water heater, and broke the valve. There were two fresh scratches on his lower back that ran parallel and about an inch apart. The valve was lying on the floor near his head. The paramedics were called to confirm what the officers already knew.

For the first couple of hours on the scene, the police, federal agents, and coroners assumed that this was a suicide. There was no gun visible anywhere near the body, but since they had not moved the body, everyone figured the gun was lying underneath. It was a contact gunshot wound through the sternum. The partly jacketed .38-caliber bullet traveled six inches into Jack's body at a thirty-degree downward angle, passed through the right atrium and ventricle of his heart, obliterated his right coronary artery, grazed his descending aorta, ricocheted off his backbone, and then came to a stop just behind his heart. Death was momentary if not immediate. Gunpowder residue was not found on his shirt, but it was present inside the gunshot wound.

When the coroner finally turned Jack's body over to prepare it for transport, the simple suicide case suddenly got complicated—there was no gun found under his body—no gun at all. It's kind of difficult to fire a fatal shot into one's own chest and then with a split second of life left, dispose of the weapon so well that a battery of investigators can't find it.

That left only a couple of options: Someone killed him or he killed himself and someone removed the gun. One possibility about a homicide remained quite clear: Jack was involved in illegal activities, and he had confederates who were also involved in illegal activities. Some of the coconspirators had already been flushed out, some had not yet, and some never would be. Could someone have been afraid enough that Jack would turn him in to go to his house and kill him? The chance seemed remote since Jack had not given any information before his death. The investigators never did seem very interested in the possibility that someone else killed him. But why would someone remove the gun?

Insurance could be one reason. A mortgage accidental death insurance policy Jack had taken out with Minnesota Mutual Life Insurance Company in March 1991—one month after he proposed to Wendy—would have paid off his heavily mortgaged house to the tune of $150,000. A second life insurance policy, issued by CUNA Mutual Insurance Group in November 1992, also carried a payoff of $150,000. But neither policy would pay a dime in a case of suicide.

Then there was the question of where the gun would have come from in the first place. Jack had a number of weapons, but the feds had confiscated all they could find. Wendy said she carried one in her car, and she produced it for the police—it was not the weapon that killed Jack. Still, someone with as many connections as Jack had could have conceivably gotten another gun from someone in the amount of time he had. The investigators looked long and hard at Wendy, interviewing her several times, but she steadfastly denied doing anything with a gun that might have been at the scene. The insurance companies, by the way, refused to pay the award on Jack's death, saying that the coroner had not ruled out suicide. Wendy filed suit against Minnesota Mutual in August 1995, claiming, in part, that the burden of proof of suicide was on the insurance company.

A couple of other aspects of Jack's death seemed to point to suicide. Why the basement? If someone was going to kill him, why would they march him at gunpoint into the basement? If it was suicide, he may have chosen the basement so Wendy would not be reminded of his death every time she was in the main part of the house. Plus there was less chance that the shooting would harm the house or that the expected hordes of cops would mess up the house by tracking in and out.

Another interesting aspect is that tests of his blood and body fluids found no alcohol, yet alcohol was found in his stomach. It takes mere minutes for alcohol to get from the stomach into the bloodstream, which means that Jack had died just a couple of minutes after taking a slug of booze. Investigators did see a bottle of bourbon on the dining room table. Might not a man who had been a longtime hard drinker take one last shot for the road before preparing to kill himself? It would certainly seem to fit.

Those are rather minute aspects next to the fact that Jack had talked about suicide so many times after he was indicted that prosecutors and psychologists considered him a suicide risk. There was also the timing of his death as compared to the timing of other events. He had broken his hip just a few days before Judge Blackburn was set to rule on his competency. He had cut himself with the chain saw just a couple of days before his trial was supposed to start. And he died a couple of days before he was to be sentenced. Anyone who believed the first two events were deliberate attempts by Jack to harm himself might believe on that basis alone that he killed himself.

Certainly no one believed that Jack was not going to be sentenced to some time in prison, and it was certainly well known that cops and judges were high-risk prisoners—popular targets in the prisons' general population. That's the physical risk on top of the sheer embarrassment of an upholder of the law having to serve out a sentence. Many a crooked cop has opted for pulling the trigger rather than being locked up.

Jack's body was cremated, and a small memorial service was held at Johns-Ridout's Southside Chapel in Birmingham on Valentine's Day, the day Jack had been scheduled to be sentenced in federal court. On that same day Attorney Greg Jones showed up in court for his scheduled sentencing. Judge Blackburn apparently saw that as an opportunity to make the public statement about Jack that she wasn't going to get to make with Jack standing before her. While sentencing Jones, she said that Jack had "faked physical and mental symptoms" to avoid prosecution and that in the end she had accepted his no-fault guilty plea because it was "in the best interest of this state that the people not hear the details of what was going on in a court where he was selling justice. He was guilty, and he knew he was guilty when he entered that plea. He pled for what reason, who knows? But he was guilty, I am convinced of it."

Jones's attorney, William Clark, objected to Blackburn's tirade, saying, "I get the feeling Jack Montgomery is being sentenced here today, not Greg Jones, because Jack Montgomery is not available." Blackburn never did reveal what sentence she had planned to give Jack.

Speaking of faked symptoms, one other interesting aspect of Jack's autopsy concerned examination of his central nervous system. Despite the defense's constant claims of diminished mental capacity, the medical examiner found only "age appropriate changes" in his brain.

A separate doctor wrote, "Patients with Alzheimer's disease always have extensive injury to the hippocampus including large numbers of senile plaques and neurofibrillary tangles. No such neuropathology is present in this case. In fact, the overall number of plaques and tangles is less than that expected for an individual of this age."

That's a lot of doctor talk, but the examiners apparently went out of their way to show there was no visible biological defect in Jack Montgomery's brain. That in itself was not proof that he had been faking, but it was another big point in favor of that theory.

About a month after Jack's death, when it seemed nothing else could happen, something else did. Warren King was killed in his home, a gunshot to the head, about two weeks before he was to begin serving his sentence in federal prison. Investigators found King's body sitting in a chair in his living room. A friend told police he had just dropped off King from the bowling alley where he spent so much of his time. King's live-in girlfriend, Regina Gratton, told police she had been asleep when King came home. She woke up the next morning, made him his breakfast, and when she tried to rouse him from the chair, she realized he was dead. She said she had not heard a gunshot.

Suddenly there were new questions and theories about Jack's death. Could someone be wiping out everyone involved in this case? There was talk about hit men from Detroit, and the conspiracy theorists were having a grand old time. Some people worried about Greg Jones's safety in federal prison, and Mark White visited Jefferson County District Attorney David Barber and talked about security measures that could be taken to protect Wendy.

In about a month, however, Birmingham police charged Gratton with capital murder, saying that she was a drug addict and had simply robbed and killed her longtime boyfriend. That seemed to put the investigators right back at the beginning on Jack's death.

Two years after King's death, Regina Gratton stood trial. Her attorneys, Doug Jones and Richard Jaffee, did their best to convince the jury that King's death and Jack Montgomery's death were more than just coincidence. They proved to the jury that King had been trying to get out of his one-year prison sentence by offering even more information about even more defendants in the bribery scheme. Someone, the attorneys argued, wanted to shut up Jack and King to keep from being prosecuted. Gratton was even warned by Brannan that he had received information about supposed hit men coming after "a woman" involved in the Jack Montgomery case.

The prosecution, led by Assistant District Attorney Laura Petro, told the jury that King was killed by his crack-addicted girlfriend, who then took his gawdy, expensive gold jewelry and pawned it for crack money. The jury deliberated nearly three days, sometimes arguing so loudly that they could be heard outside of the jury room, and came back hopelessly deadlocked. A mistrial was declared. Apparently Jones and Jaffee had muddied the waters just enough.

Within a week or so of Jack's death, Mark White, filed a motion in federal court, asking Blackburn to wipe the slate clean—void all charges that had been filed against Jack and his subsequent guilty plea—because he died before the proceedings could be completed. The idea that Jack could be declared an innocent man when it was so obvious that he was not innocent rubbed a lot of people the wrong way. The irony was plenty thick though—he had to die to be cleared. Blackburn took her time with the motion, more than a year, in fact. The whole thing obviously repulsed her, but the case law, as she pointed out in her opinion, was clear: Jack Montgomery had to be cleared of all charges.

"The prevailing view in the federal courts, including the Eleventh U.S. Circuit Court of Appeals, is that criminal proceedings must be abated where a defendant dies while an appeal of his conviction is pending," she wrote. She cited the U.S. Supreme Court decision in *Durham v. United States,* which said, in part, "The lower federal courts were unanimous on the rule to be applied: Death pending direct review of a criminal conviction abates not only the appeal but also all proceedings had in the prosecution from its inception."

In Jack Montgomery's case, Blackburn said, the rule might not seem to apply since it was usually applied in cases that are on appeal. "Although his guilty plea was, in itself, a conviction," she wrote, "Jack Montgomery was never sentenced. Because a defendant has the right to be present at his sentencing, the court cannot sentence Montgomery posthumously. As a general rule, the appellate courts have no jurisdiction over a criminal action until there has been a final judgment, that is, until the defendant has been convicted and sentenced."

As of May 1995, when Blackburn issued the order, Jack Montgomery became an innocent man in the eyes of the law. The law that he had served, scorned, and prostituted had, in the end, worked for him.

Blackburn, however, did not miss the chance to spit on Jack's grave. "If the process cannot be followed to its last possible breath, then it shall be ended and the slate wiped clean. Jack Montgomery's reputation shall enjoy no such privilege, however, in spite of what happens to his criminal record. His disgrace and ignominious death may be the only aspects of his existence that survive in the public memory. His name will continue to carry a stain of corruption.

"After hearing the evidence in the trial of Jack Montgomery's codefendant, Greg Jones, this court is convinced that Montgomery put justice on the auction block and thereby made a mockery of the high office with which the public had entrusted him. He defiled that office, and betrayed the people's trust, for the love of money. Public infamy seems an inadequate consequence for his wrongdoing."

EPILOGUE

Agent Steve Brannan continued to investigate the Jack Montgomery bribery conspiracy, and his efforts yielded indictments of two more lawyers. The first was Tony Falletta, who was indicted in May 1994 on a total of eleven counts of extortion, tampering with witnesses, money laundering, and income-tax evasion. The unusual aspect of this case was that Warren King was not involved. Falletta, the prosecution charged, committed extortion directly in concert with Jack. Once again people wondered about the legal community in Birmingham. OK, Falletta had been a marked man since his previous conviction and disbarment, but what about the other lawyers who were close to Jack? How many more would be indicted? How many more should be but wouldn't be?

Falletta was tried in late July. Tarrant Police Detective Warren Reno finally got to tell a jury his tale about drug dealer Jessie Struggs and how Jack started pulling the same stunt with him that he did later with Hoover Police Department Detective Mark Hobbs. The prosecution alleged that Jack was tampering with the Struggs case because Falletta had extorted money from Struggs for the favors. Other Jefferson County judges testified that the kind of ex parte contact that Falletta had with Jack was at the very least unethical.

Drug dealer Eric Walker testified that he had paid Falletta as much as $40,000 because Falletta had promised to get Jack to give him a light sentence. Brannan was able to tape-record conversations between Walker and Falletta about the bribes, despite the fact that the investigation into Jack Montgomery had been public knowledge for some time and Falletta knew that his name had come up in the investigation. Frankly, Falletta was not known as a mental giant.

The jury also heard from Thurman Eugene Moore II and his father. Both testified that they sold everything the family had in order to pay Falletta the $50,000 he said he needed to guarantee that charges of purse snatching and drug possession against Thurman II would go away. Part of the money was supposed to go to a judge, the father and son testified.

During the trial Falletta's family members approached reporters and tried to convince them to write their stories a little more favorably for the defendant. One day several priests showed up in the courtroom and sat on the defense side of the gallery. Obviously Falletta wanted the jury to see that he had God on his side. But it took the jury only five hours to find Falletta guilty on six counts. He was sentenced to three years in a federal prison and fined $15,000.

Then in November 1995 Attorney Jesse Shotts was indicted on five counts of bribery, fifteen counts of mail fraud, one count of mail fraud conspiracy, and six counts of obstructing justice. When Shotts's trial rolled around in February 1996, Mike Rasmussen told the jurors that Shotts owned and operated a bail bond business, despite the fact that Alabama state law precluded lawyers from having any financial interest in a bail bond operation. That infraction did not come under federal jurisdiction, but Shotts's use of the U.S. mail to procure licenses for the bail bond business under false pretenses did.

One of the scams being run by Shotts's bail bond business, Rasmussen testified, was getting Jack to sign stacks and stacks of blank bonds. Later when Shotts's employees filled out the bonds and charged clients the usual fee, the business did not have to put its own assets on the line because the bond was signed by a judge. That made it a recognizance bond, which the defendant should not have had to pay for if it had been issued legitimately. At J.C. Bail Bonds, the signed blank bonds were called "Jack bonds," Rasmussen told the jury.

Shotts's defense centered largely on proving that some of the government's witnesses were drug users and fornicators. Somehow that didn't seem to shock the jurors. After less than a day of deliberations, they found Shotts guilty of all but the extortion counts. Apparently Rasmussen's inability to prove Shotts had placed cash in Jack Montgomery's hands in exchange for the Jack bonds left open enough reasonable doubt for the jury to find Shotts not guilty on those counts.

Since it was widely known that Shotts had breakfast at Jack Montgomery's house the day of Jack's death, it was speculated among the courthouse crowd that the prosecution was hoping to get something out of Shotts about Jack's death. If the attorney knew something about Jack's death, surely he would tell all after being convicted and looking at prison time in addition to losing his license to practice law.

But Jack's death remained a mystery.

Wendy filed suit against both CUNA Mutual Insurance Group and Minnesota Mutual Life Insurance Company, the two companies that held Jack's mortgage insurance policies, but neither company wanted to pay because suicide had not been ruled out as the cause of Jack's death. Wendy and her attorneys claimed that the burden was on the insurance companies to prove that Jack's death was a suicide.

CUNA settled with Wendy, but Minnesota Mutual preferred to go to trial. Among the documents filed by Minnesota Mutual in response to Wendy's suit was a report by Dr. Brian Frist, an associate medical examiner from Atlanta. Based on his studies of the coroner's report and photographs from the autopsy and death scene, Frist asserted that Jack might have been holding a gun when he died, and he wrote, "It appears that the right hand may have been used to hold the weapon and pull the trigger with the thumb finger." The case came to trial in early 1997, and Wendy lost.

Jefferson County's Chief Deputy Coroner Jay Glass had examined Jack's body and the scene the day of Jack's death. When he heard about Frist's report, Glass replied, "It just goes to show that you can find someone to say anything you want them to, as long as you pay them." Glass did not agree or disagree with Frist's assertion that Jack killed himself. He did, however, adamantly disagree with Frist's drawing conclusions from the position of Jack's hand. "You can't tell anything from that," Glass said. "The man fell. He hit his head. The impact on the floor could have caused his hand and fingers to end up in any number of positions."

Many people wondered aloud about the results of gunpowder residue tests on Jack's hand. Glass said that such tests are no longer used because they simply are not reliable. The absence of gunpowder does not indicate anything for sure, and the presence of gunpowder has the same effect.

On December 17, 1995, *The Birmingham News* ran a long feature about the area's more famous unsolved murders, and it included Jack's death, even though it had occurred almost two years earlier. Among some of the crazier theories the story reported being bandied about were the dog theory and the balloon theory. According to the dog theory, Jack killed himself with a gun that was tied to his dog's collar. The shot scared the dog, and he ran out of the basement with the gun. A short time later the gun fell off, and the dog buried it.

According to the balloon theory, Jack shot himself with a gun that was tied to a helium balloon that floated off to who-knows-where, which ignores the fact that Jack died in his basement. How could the balloon have gotten out?

For most people the mystery of Jack's death, like the enigma of his life, became the subject of good sport. And like any good legend, the tales of Jack Montgomery continue to enjoy life long after the man himself enjoyed life.

Anyone who is familiar with the history of the Wild West or with Paul Newman movies has heard the name Roy Bean. Born sometime around 1825 in the hills of Kentucky, Bean went on to join the ranks of the people who were Wild West legends, even before his death in 1903. The West had its famous bandits and lawmen, and Bean was its most famous judge. Actually, as with any other legendary figure of that era, it's not exactly clear if Bean was famous or infamous, but ordinary people were fascinated by his exploits.

What qualified Bean for notoriety was the way he adhered to conventions only when it benefited him. When it didn't, he merely made up his own rules. Bean never went to law school. He was barely literate. His decisions would not have stood up to any kind of constitutional scrutiny, and more often than not, he literally robbed defendants and then sentenced them. But he had a way of keeping the peace and making people feel as though justice had been done in a place where law and order meant little.

At the age of fifty-six Bean had left his family and sought fame and fortune by following the progress of the railroad through West Texas. Before long he settled on the west bank of the Pecos River, within spitting distance of Mexico, and set up a saloon under a tent. Among the migrant railroad workers, gamblers, and thieves that made up the population of those encampments, old Roy Bean seemed like a pretty stable guy. The Texas Rangers assigned to the area liked Bean and his saloon and soon started bringing the people they arrested in for judgment since the nearest court was hundreds of miles away.

In 1882 Roy Bean was officially made a justice of the peace. Always one to hold up a dollar and declare it to be a fortune, Bean dubbed himself to be the "Law West of the Pecos" on a large sign hung outside his saloon.

It did not take long for stories about this rough-and-tumble judge with a potbelly, white whiskers, and sombrero to travel across the plains and sometimes wind up in the newspapers. In those early days one defendant charged in Bean's court brought a young lawyer with him. Every time Judge Bean said something, the lawyer objected, and every time Bean overruled him. Finally Bean threatened to hang the barrister right there in the saloon. The lawyer thought about it for a moment and then decided to drop the case.

Most of the time, though, the positions of prosecutor and attorney for the defense were usually handled by whichever customers happened to be in the place and were sober enough to conduct themselves without throwing Bean into a lather. Juries were threatened with jail unless they arrived at some verdict. It was a kangaroo court run by thieves and drunks, but it served a purpose.

Sometimes Judge Roy Bean's decisions simply stretched common sense. For instance, when one young man was brought to him on a charge of carrying a concealed weapon, Bean pondered for a moment and then ruled that if the man was arrested while standing still, he couldn't be carrying anything—and if he was moving, then he was traveling, and it was legal for travelers to carry weapons. Bean dismissed the case.

The most famous of Judge Bean's decisions was for an Irishman who was brought to Roy's court on charges of murdering a Chinese man. Bean hemmed and hawed, ruminated, and thumbed through his law book. Finally he declared that he had read through all of the statutes of the State of Texas and found that while killing a human being was against the law, "There ain't a damned line in it nowheres that makes it illegal to kill a Chinaman. The defendant is discharged."

As well as serving as the judge for the area, Roy Bean also served as the coroner—and he always made tracks when someone told him of a dead body because each coroner's inquest was worth $5, payable by the state. One time a fellow named Pat O'Brien fell off the bridge over Myers Canyon. Bean had the body brought to the saloon and placed on a table. He searched the corpse for some form of identification, and, in so doing, found a pistol and $40. He promptly fined the late Pat O'Brien $40 for carrying a concealed weapon, and history still remembers Roy Bean as the judge who fined a dead man.

Both Roy Bean and Jack Montgomery meted out justice on their own terms—Bean because he didn't know any better, Jack because he knew better but thought his way best. Both men believed that the bigger they were in people's minds, the better they could make their judgments stick. Both men were hard and callous but sometimes capable of charity.

Jack had heard himself being compared to Roy Bean and rather relished the comparison. By reputation he knew Bean to have been a rugged individualist, much like he wished to be known.

Jack Montgomery and Roy Bean had substantial bravado and more than their fair share of quirks, but there is a substantial difference. While Bean was more of a desperado than Jack ever dreamed of being, Bean was embraced not only by history but also by his contemporaries because to many he symbolized the rough-and-ready times and the godless country he lived in.

Jack Montgomery, however, stuck out like a peacock in a chicken yard. For a while he was a diversion from his times. Eventually, though, the very thing that made Bean more of a "character" brought Jack to his knees. His contemporaries judged him harshly, and history is unlikely to be much kinder.

INDEX

About the Author

Steve Joynt, a native of Richmond, received his under-graduate degree in American government and English literature from the University of Virginia in 1984 and his master's degree in journalism from Columbia University in 1985. Steve joined the *Birmingham* (Alabama) *Post-Herald* staff in 1985 and has won the Scripps Howard Newswriter of the Year award three times. He won the Alabama Associated Press Newswriting Sweep-stakes award in 1993 and was named to the Scripps Howard Editorial Hall of Fame in 1994.

Steve and his wife, Nancy, live in Shelby County, Alabama.